GOLF – THE TRUE STORY

Books by Steve McGregor

The Bruce Novels (in chronological order)
- Adventures of a Jackeroo
- The Adventures of Bruce from Bondi
- Golf – The True Story

GOLF
THE TRUE STORY

Written & illustrated by
Steve McGregor

Steve McGregor Books

This is a work of fiction. Names, characters, places, and incidents either are the product of the author's imagination or are used fictitiously. Any resemblance to actual persons, living or dead, events, or locales is entirely coincidental.

ISBN 978-0-646-85003-0

Copyright © Steve McGregor, 2021

All rights reserved. No part of this publication may be reproduced, stored in a retrieval system, or transmitted in any form or by any means, electronic, mechanical, photocopying, recording, or otherwise, without the prior permission of the copyright owner.

Dedicated to
Garry Webb, Owen Thomas and all the keen golfers

GOLF – THE TRUE STORY

PREFACE..1
1 A BRIEF HISTORY OF GOLF 1
2 HISTORY OF THE GOLF BALL 39
3 DESIGNING A NEW GOLF BALL 44
4 PSYCHOLOGICAL PROFILING 48
5 THE EQUIPMENT 56
6 DESIGNING ALTERNATE GOLF GEAR............ 68
7 THE GOLF SWINGS 79
8 GOLF TERMINOLOGY 90
9 PEOPLE WHO PLAY GOLF 102

10 SOME OTHER GOLFER TYPES 139

11 THE PRO SHOP 144

12 MENTAL ATTITUDE 147

13 PROBLEM SHOTS 152

14 DISTRACTIONS IN GOLF 162

15 THE 19TH HOLE 174

"Golf is deceptively simple and endlessly complicated." – Arnold Palmer

PREFACE

"They call it golf because all the other four-letter words were taken." – Raymond Floyd

The author chose to read a book on how to be better at golf rather than play.

Guess how many books have been written on the subject of golf. Don't you know? Give up? Well, I don't know either. There is one thing I do know, however, and that is that no one, possibly, has written a book quite like this one.

This book is filled with humorous observations and funny illustrations, for I am a firm believer in the age-old axiom that *a picture is worth a thousand words.*

Also, if you have read any of my other books like *The Adventures of a Jackeroo* and *The Adventures of Bruce from Bondi* then you'll already be familiar with *this* book's hero 'Bruce.'

I mention Bruce many times throughout, for he (like me) enjoys the esteemed and noble game of golf. Having lived a rich and colourful life firstly as a jackaroo, amongst the heat and flies of Enngonia (West NSW); as a trainee hotel manager, at the Auckland Hotel in Bondi; and later as a real estate agent; he now, in retirement, enjoys sharing all he knows about the game with you, the reader.

I, like Bruce, have been a golfer now for many years and I am still waiting to be good at it. Nowadays, as my hands and knees start to ache, I find myself *writing* about the game more often than I play it.

Not willing to accept the possibility that I might be a dud golfer though, I nevertheless persevere. I confess that *in my mind* I still hold out hope that one day I'll be a champion. However, it's when I hit the ball that all my imaginings come unstuck.

I watch other golfers and professionals play the game on television, and they make it look so darn easy. And I dwell on my shortcomings. *Why can't I make the ball soar like that,* I think. *It can't all be my fault.* That is why 'Chapter 6: Designing

Alternate Golf Gear' is so important. Maybe someone out there will come up with a *new* game, a game that will allow different alternate designs in golf equipment, hitherto outlawed (or deemed non-conforming) which will make all the difference for hacks like me.

There are many pointers in this handy little book that will help the beginner golfer, gifted amateur, or even the professional. Enjoy the book and don't get caught in a hazard!

1

A BRIEF HISTORY OF GOLF

"Golf can best be defined as an endless series of tragedies obscured by the occasional miracle." – Anonymous

It was a Sunday and Bruce was lying back on the sofa by the fire. Outside the rain was bucketing down and he knew, with a sinking heart, that his golf day was ruined.

All week he had been looking forward to seeing his mates for a golf game and then afterward have a few cold ones at the clubhouse to finish off a glorious day.

All he could say to himself was, "Jeez, it's just not fair." Yes, Bruce was feeling rather sorry for himself. Being retired was hard to handle. After working in the real estate game, firstly as a salesman and then having his own business, for nigh on forty years, Bruce was feeling the withdrawal symptoms of sitting around and doing nothing.

He sipped on his port wine and brandy as his mind drifted to his favourite pastime. Years ago he went through a stage of being interested in history and now his mind, fuelled

GOLF – THE TRUE STORY

by the potent drink, was ranging far and wide as to the origins of the game. His favourite game - golf.

The historians lead you to believe that the game of golf only began in Holland (as it was then named), in the 15th century, and was then imported by some deluded souls to a wet and misty country called Scotland.

From Bruce's research, he has been able to ascertain that the game of golf was played long before that, although it may have faded out of history after the Ice Age. However, a game such as this was bound to be reborn by other stalwart fellows and it continues to this day, albeit in a different form.

The evidence of the earliest golfer that Bruce has been able to locate in the various obscure papers written by anthropologists and archaeologists is that of Stone Age man. No doubt the game was also carried on through the Bronze Age and adapted by the players of the Iron Age.

Later the Ancient Egyptians took advantage of their country's sandy terrain and the game of golf flourished. Naturally, when the Romans invaded Egypt they were at first surprised and then astounded as to how challenging the game of golf could be. And we all know how the Romans liked a challenge.

The Pax Romana was to flourish for nigh on a thousand years and during that time the Roman way of life was adopted by many of the peoples who were living under the yoke of the Legions.

Eventually, the Roman Empire fell and many of the ways of life were still carried on by the people of what is now called Europe. Everywhere that the Roman Legions marched you would find evidence of golf courses, usually adjacent to the towns. Regrettably, the courses were allowed to deteriorate over the centuries and the game of golf languished in the Dark Ages.

However, human nature as it is Bruce found evidence of a resurgence of golf. Even the Vikings, in the cold North, had taken up the game and had become quite proficient at it. When they invaded England, France, where Normandy is now located, and even Russia, the game of golf was played by the wealthy of those lands.

Sometimes a prince would be taken to task by his king for neglecting his studies and practicing combat. Swordsmanship and the art of war would take second place to the addictive game of hitting a small ball and chasing after it.

The Netherlands had taken on the game and their oddly shaped flattened ball was hit to skim across the ice of their ponds. When the Scots discovered the game they added some innovations.

The name of the Scotsman who decided to have a putting green and a hole in the ground to hit the ball into has long been forgotten. Never the less this added nuance to the game resulted in an exciting and sometimes frustrating few hours. Just imagine hairy Gaelic-speaking lads smashing golf balls and frightening the ladies with their language as they sliced their ball into the heather.

Every so often the English would take it upon themselves to invade Scotland, as a few kings had found the taste of whisky to their liking. It was only a short step from invasion to the acquisition of the small distilleries dotted around the highlands. Naturally while sipping on their wee dram or two the English were surprised to see small groups of kilted Scotsmen, with light clubs hitting small balls around and uttering vile oaths.

The English must have thought that looked like fun, that is, seeing all these Scotsmen looking up into the sky and shouting and waving their fists because they too started playing the game. It wasn't long before they had a brilliant plan. The plan turned into a campaign and armies marched to and fro across the heather. These 'troubles' ended up having the English ban the Scots from playing golf. Why? Well, firstly the English hated seeing the Scots enjoying themselves and secondly, the English didn't want too much competition.

The Welsh did not play golf either. Their national sport was eating leeks and tin mining and this did not give them too much time to play anything, let alone play the game of golf.

The great empire builders, the English, over time introduced the game of golf to other countries in the British Empire. It did not seem to flourish though as cricket seemed to gain more popularity. The one exception was in the new world where one of the main benefits of British rule in the Colonies was the introduction of golf.

The Americans eventually became so good at the game that the British tried to ban it and we all know what happened then. The American War of Independence in 1775 of course!

The Italians were not always permitted to play on the golf courses and usually, the local Don and his henchmen would play. Oddly the Don would always win the game and if he looked like losing, then the golf balls or even fellow players would mysteriously go missing.

Bruce often tells the yarn about one of his mates of Italian heritage. He likes to call himself Barry, to fit in and avoid the fact that he was Italian. However, his mother would provide him with a snack every time he played golf. While Barry's mates were tucking into a pie or a peanut butter sandwich washed down with a dose of orangeade, Barry was spooning a mixture of spaghetti and meatballs while sipping on a glass of Chianti. Lucky Benedetto.

Now, the Spaniards are something when it comes to golf. They just don't. Their whole history of conquest saw that the Spaniards and their deep abiding quest for gold ensured that not many conquistadors took up the game of golf. Anyhow, the Inquisition would have put a stop to all that, as they had outlawed games of any kind along with sport. But the Inquisition did command that all attend church on a Sunday, all day, and that ruled out one-seventh of the week where a Spaniard could play the game.

The Greeks, alas, were usually too poor to play golf. The only good ground on those dry islands or the mainland was devoted to growing food and so the number of golf courses was at a minimum. It was said that Alexander the Great was a top golfer and the 'Great' in his name was due to a particular game where he had all of the 18 holes in one. Of course, that may just be mythology but Bruce thinks it may have something to do with Alexander being a tyrant and anyone who looked like beating Alexander, was sent off to fight the Scythian people or some such place of danger where if you had any luck, you would only last a season or two.

Now, seeing we are taking a swipe at most of the countries of the world, let's move on to the Hungarians. The reason why they are not great golfers is that their breakfasts of Hungarian Goulash, if you don't mind, rest heavily on their stomachs and so they spend a lot of their time digesting the stuff. Playing golf at the same time would be too difficult. Anyhow, they could never get anyone to translate the rules of golf into Hungarian and that didn't help the popularity of golf in that country.

All of this potted history aside, the following pages deals in some depth with the history of golf through the ages. Naturally, not all can be mentioned here although the main stages of golf's history are dealt with.

THE STONE AGE 7000 B.C.

"My swing is so bad, I look like a caveman killing his lunch." – Lee Trevino

Anthropologists had long been puzzled over various images appearing on cave paintings by ancient man. The slim club-like implements, once thought a kind of weapon, had been observed. It was only when an obscure and hitherto overlooked part of the famous Lascaux Cave painting was illuminated by modern LED lights was the mystery solved.

Experts estimated after testing that the remains were buried some 15,000 years ago. They then identified the nature of the club-like weapons. To the surprise of the researchers and staff, they were identified as golf clubs rather than as weapons. These findings show that ancient man did have time for leisure and was not a brute always on the hunt for food.

As you know, this book is written by Bruce Thompson who inhabited earlier books such as "Adventures of a Jackeroo" and "The Adventures of Bruce from Bondi". He has long speculated that golf was a far more ancient game than previously thought and the findings contained in this book, *"Golf – The True Story"* shows what he has been researching for many years.

It can be assumed that the Cro-Magnon man would occasionally neglect his prime role of hunting for food. It can be assumed that the womenfolk of the tribe would be angry and complain that the hunter spent too much time hitting the ball instead of hunting for game.

Bruce dryly chuckled when he read about these findings and also thought that nothing much has changed during the last fifteen thousand years or so.

GOLF – THE TRUE STORY

The huntsman enjoyed a game of leisure. Hunting could be worrying.

He would promise to only play on the weekends but despite his best endeavours, he would always sneak a game or two in during the week. And this made his woman mad.

Archaeologists have long thought that their golf clubs would have been fashioned from a fire-hardened shaft of wood with a carved head of walrus or deer antler. All were affixed by resin or sinew. Balls would probably have been water-worn pebbles that could have been wrapped in animal skin.

The tribes would have been small, perhaps no more than seven men of hunting age excluding the young and the aged. Of the seven hunters possibly two may have been interested in pursuing the pastime of hitting a round ball with their 'golf club'.

These ancient men, due to their well-muscled torsos, would be able to wield great power, and therein lay a problem. The ball would always be hit a great distance but when it came to putting or their short game, they were not great. They still hit the ball too far.

Eventually, the very strong Stone-Age players learned not to hit the ball so far. The sheer effort in trying to find their balls ensured that they spent most of their time hunting around and grunting away. Nothing much has changed has it.

Anyhow the game flourished on the tundra in the North of the Asian continent and on the prairies of North America. The Savanna in Africa was a different matter due to the number of predatory animals lurking to pounce on any prey, including any early man that became too intent on looking at the ground. The early golf players on the continent of Africa therefore died out as all those who showed any aptitude for the game of golf were taken and the gene pool, therefore, became extinct for golf-type man.

GOLF – THE TRUE STORY

The same issues were encountered on the pampas of South America as the Jaguar was king on the grasslands, not early golf players. The balance between the game flourishing and its extinction went on for thousands of years and despite the depredations of the carnivores survived until it was found to have cropped up in ancient Egypt.

THE ANCIENT EGYPTIANS 2500 BC

"I think I am going to need a bigger sand wedge." – Pharaoh

The Egyptians lived in a land where it was only fertile alongside a pretty big river. The rest of the country was sand, in fact, it was a very large sand trap or bunker.

Pharaoh knew that to be a good golfer he should build another statue, of himself.

As with today, there is not too much time for having fun or playing games in Egypt but Pharaoh and his cohorts welcomed the chance to have a round of golf or two.

If you look closely; paintings and carvings on many buildings show various nobles with golfing equipment. Those large flail-like poles were no doubt used by the Egyptians to deal with any asps that were lurking around.

The design of the golf club was perfected here as hitherto a club was a tool to do anything, whether it be a drive, lob, or a putt. (Not much has changed here according to Bruce in relation to his game).

The sand wedge had evolved in Egypt and in the main was the only club used by the Egyptians. Putting in all that sand would have been a drag in more ways than one. The Egyptians soon learned to seek out areas in the desert where the ground was harder and with less sand. This then led to a completely different game and in the Eighth Dynasty one of the ancients, who was an engineer, designed and perfected a golf club that would hit the ball further.

The Ptolemaic Dynasty saw the occupation of Egypt and the eventual takeover when Cleopatra VII Philopator was the Pharaoh. She was the last of a great line of golfers who had to put up with a lot as the Romans, by now, had occupied her favourite golf course.

All this worry and the loss of her golf course may have resulted in her death. It was later found that she died on the golf course from an asp bite when one of her slaves missed flailing the creature and it reared up and fastened its fangs in her breast.

The Romans were saddened by the passing of a popular Pharaoh and decided to do the best they could by allowing Caesar, the then ruler of Rome, to become Pharaoh and carry on the good work. It is also assumed that when

GOLF – THE TRUE STORY

Rome conquered Egypt the game was adopted by Caesar and his tribunes and exported back home.

THE ROMANS 58 BC

"Veni, Vidi, Vici, - I came, I saw, I conquered. I had a hole in one." – Julius Caesar.

Now, by the year 58 BC, you will find Julius Caesar and many of his fellow Romans with a golf club in their hands instead of a Gladius (sword).

Caesar was a successful politician, a faultless soldier and a champion golfer.

Julius Caesar was a very busy man. He played hard and fought hard and most probably loved hard, but that is another story. Wars, pitched battles, intrigue in politics, and troubles at home with his shrew of a wife, were all grist to the mill for Caesar. However, he often said that the game of 'sphera propellentibus' (Latin for ball pushing) was potentially more dangerous than any other trial or tribulation that he had ever experienced.

Ball Hitting (nowadays called Golf) was played for high stakes in ancient Rome. If an enemy tribe or nation, for that matter, dared to defy Rome then the Legions would get out their gladius and hack off a few enemy heads.

After the battles, a picked squad of Legionaries would get out their golf clubs and then hit the severed heads around the Colosseum or various other amphitheatres throughout the Empire. The Plebeians particularly enjoyed this spectacle and followed their champions as to who could hit a head the furthest.

Playing the game with many of his Senator pal's mates was also fraught with peril. Caesar would spend half of his nervous energy wondering if he would survive the game before one of his supposed friends would assassinate him. Despite all this worry, Caesar was looking forward to his next game of his favourite pastime and he asked his secretary to ensure that he was available for a game in the Ides of March. Now, his golfing partner Brutus was very angry. Caesar had reneged on playing a game of golf with his mates that weekend and Brutus was sore. In fact he was more than sore he was murderous. Romans were known for their pride and Brutus had it in bucket loads. He was so angry that he missed out on his game of golf that he vowed to dissolve his golf partnership forthwith. He knew though that to do that to his ex-friend Caesar was a dangerous plan and he invited a few of his friends to join in for a bit of bloodletting.

GOLF – THE TRUE STORY

Amongst playing golf and war a little bit of bloodletting was a Roman's favourite pastime. Brutus and his mates met one fateful morning and waylaid Julius Caesar on his way to the Senate building. Brutus greeted Caesar and before he could reply knives were rising and falling and Caesar's white purple-lined toga was splashed with blood.

As you can see, the Romans took the game of golf very seriously. One must never forget though that the Roman Empire had its influence in many things. Be they politics, building, war, or sport. The combat of the gladiators was fun and even more so when the favourites survived the bloodletting. The game of golf too was right up there in the popularity stakes. Consequently, when Augustus came to power the game took on a new dimension. It became more popular than ever.

Golf was played by all manner of people. The slaves had games where more than twenty were hooking and slicing away with gay abandon. The golf clubs were rough and ready but the game was enjoyed by all.

The Plebeians also played the game of golf and their clubs and balls were of excellent design. The cheaper clubs had bronze heads but they still did their job.

The Patricians though had it really good. They played the game in luxury. Some clubs were embellished with gold and the slaves were expected to carry all the kit as well as supplies and provisions for the after-game orgy. The orgy was most probably a lot more fun than our 19th hole, back at the clubhouse, but that is where the tradition has stemmed from.

> *"Aggressive play is a vital asset of the world's greatest golfers. However, it's even more important to the average player. Attack this game in a bold, confident and determined way, and you'll make a*

> *giant leap toward realizing your full potential as a player."* - Greg Norman

THE VIKINGS 950 AD

> *"When you go golfing remember to take your battle axe." Arne* – The Berserker

The Roman Empire influenced so much in so many countries of the ancient world and as with many conquerors, they made sure that the people of the conquered lands adopted their culture and traditions.

However, far away from the sunny Mediterranean Sea in the cold and dark countries where the Norse lived, even though they were not part of the Roman Empire, they too adopted many of Rome's customs.

There have been few records of the way in which the Norse led their lives in the Viking era. It was the discovery of ancient graves on a lonely island that made the story a little bit clearer.

In the era of the Viking raids, which lasted about 300 years, from the late 8th century to 1066, most historians have speculated that the Vikings did not have much leisure time.

Thus, when the graves were discovered and then opened, archaeologists found more than they bargained for. This time not only did they find the usual corroded weapons, shields and armour but they found what looked like thin wooden clubs. Naturally, the wood had long since rotted but traces of their shape were observed pressed into the earth. Alongside the weapons were several stone balls and these also long mystified archaeologists as to what purpose they were used.

GOLF – THE TRUE STORY

Ragnar believed that Valhalla could wait, golf was more fun.

One theory was that they had been used by the armed warriors for their slings, an ancient but deadly weapon. The balls, mainly fashioned from a very hard stone like granite, would have been a fearsome projectile. These mysterious balls had long been studied and it was thought that they were not sling projectiles but crudely fashioned balls for a game of some kind.

This then led the experts to think that the strange club, that had been found, may have been an early form of golf club. Which inturn meant that the balls were being used in the game and were not, as first thought, ammunition for weapons. These findings then led the experts to believe that unlike earlier thinking the Vikings indeed had leisure time and played all manner of games and sports.

Later the runes, Viking writing, carved in some marker stones, showed evidence of the game of golf. It is an easy leap in thinking, therefore that once the Vikings returned home after a raid they would, as soon as they were able, spend time hitting golf balls alongside the many fjords and waterways of their land.

One can imagine that the golf games of the warlike Norse were far more deadly than the golf game, as we know it, today. The players would fail to divest themselves of all their weapons. Human nature does not change and so the motto is never make a Viking golfer angry lest they swing at you with their battle-axe instead of a golf club. Just imagine the sight of a group of golfers swinging war axes and swords, reeking of pickled herring and uttering vile oaths. All in the day of a golf game.

Because of the lack of level land in the lands of the Norse, it is theorised that the game did not comprise long shots - you just could not afford to hook your ball on their narrow fairways. Long water hazards called fjords were located adjacent to all the golf courses in the Viking era.

We can therefore assume that the golf club was shaped more like a croquet mallet and the game consisted of short hits. The balls too may have been fashioned from a hard stone and then covered with a piece of leather and sewn to hold it in place. These would have been quite sufficient and more than serve their purpose.

Despite the invasion and occupation of Britain the Vikings mysteriously did not introduce the popular game into their new lands. Scholars have debated why, and the consensus seems to be that the Vikings either did not wish to share the popular game with the Anglo-Saxon peoples or they killed off too many who may have been able to play.

THE EUROPEANS 1400S

"Winning at golf or battle, it's all the same to me." – Edward the Black Prince

In 1415 oddly enough Bruce found the first mention of golf. The place was in France and the English King Henry V was camped with his ragged army near a town called Agincourt. The French Army was there just across the paddock and there were a lot of them, in fact, so many that Henry and his generals despaired that they would ever see the next day and live to return to the wet and misty hills and dales of England. Fearful of their defeat by the huge French forces arraigned against him Henry V spoke to his troops to give them hope of victory.

His famous words though, as quoted by the bard William Shakespeare, had been misquoted, as is the usual thing in the heat of battle. The thrilling words "A horse, a horse a kingdom for a horse" was incorrect as at the time Henry was referring to his desire to be anywhere except Agincourt. He actually said, "A course, a course, a kingdom for a course" as

After Agincourt Henry V could not wait to get back home and play a round of golf.

he was referring to his favourite pastime of golf, rather than his usual wenching and carousing. King Henry would rather be playing golf than being in France at the mercy of the French knights who were keen to chop his head off and make sport with it as a soccer ball. He was no fool old Henry. Also by an odd quirk of fate a distant relation of Henry's, Richard III was to echo almost the same words, when he saw his last battle turn against him.

The subsequent battle of Henry's at Agincourt was a complete turn-around and the English army was victorious. Henry was so relieved he could not wait to get back home for a few rounds of golf.

Some forty years later in 1450, Europe was still experiencing turbulent times. The savant Leonardo da Vinci had embarked upon a series of drawings illustrating the game of golf. These pen and ink drawings depicted various ways in which golf clubs and golf balls should be designed. His marvellous series of sketches was later given the title of Golf Cursus Codex.

Meanwhile, in Germany, Johannes Gutenberg had laboured long and hard and eventually succeeded, after obtaining a loan, to build the world's first printing machine. His experiments with firstly carving wooden type and then later making them from lead, mechanical moveable type to be exact, resulted in the world's first printed book, The Holy Bible.

What is not known, according to Bruce's research, is that Gutenberg had embarked upon a second book, which was to be the world's first golf manual. This incorporated the magnificent drawings of Leonardo's Golf Cursus Codex. In these days, before the laws of copyright, Gutenberg seemed to have got away with it. However, when da Vinci, far away in Italy, heard that Gutenberg had used his Golf Codex without permission, and no remuneration to him, he was enraged.

He let his bitter feelings be known to his local confessor priest who broke the vows of the confession and scurried off to his local bishop to tell him of the evil book being printed in Germany. The Bishop spoke with his Cardinal and in no time the Inquisition was brought in to give their valued advice of what to do with the sinful book. The Inquisition was committed to ensuring that no one had any fun, and this book on a game, a game called Golf, was immediately deemed to be sinful in the extreme.

The Inquisition sent off by the fastest means possible, a delegation of Inquisitors who some weeks later arrived in Mainz and made their way to Johannes Gutenberg's house. On knocking they gained admittance to his house and were directed to his printing works adjacent to his kitchen out the back of his home.

There they stormed in and saw Gutenberg and his assistant labouring away printing a book. They quickly scanned some pages and saw the text with the wonderful drawings of Da Vinci's golf equipment. Their cries of horror were almost drowned out by the barking of Fido, Johannes's Bull Mastiff, who had smelt the unwashed bodies of the Inquisitors and was trying to clear his nostrils. After whacking the dog on the head with part of Gutenberg's printing press, and thus stilling the racket, the horrified Inquisitors demanded that Gutenberg cease production of the golf manual immediately.

They shouted that the Inquisition could not have such a book circulated amongst the common man, and it was also definitely not fit for the clergy either. The result was that the Inquisition's man on the spot fervently believed that the book would prove to be too much fun and was therefore evil. It would be too great a temptation and many of their churchgoers would not attend religious services and then be out and about on a Sunday playing golf.

In no time the moveable type and all printed pages were consequently confiscated and the head Inquisitor ominously threatened to return and prosecute Gutenberg further.

Thus the first Golf Manual was carried away to the local abbey. History now records that all Gutenberg's wonderful

GOLF – THE TRUE STORY

work had been destroyed. There was no evidence of these books and the set type to be found and it is assumed that they were either burned or buried. Never to be seen again.

THE DUTCH 1600S

> *"Act normal, as that's crazy enough."* – Old Dutch saying

Just imagine that you are stuck in Holland during winter and when you open your front door you are met by icy blasts raging across the snow-clad fields while the dikes pile the snow up in monstrous snowdrifts. The ponds are frozen and the people skate to get around or huddle beside their foot warmers munching on dried tulips or raw herrings.

Luckily Hendrik and Wilhelm brought a lantern - midday was still rather dark.

Kolf (or kolven) involved the hitting of a ball-like object with a club or mallet-type instrument. It was a sport with many of the characteristics of golf, but it was played on ice. The ball or puck would have skidded across the ice (like in ice hockey) rather than be lobbed.

On these ice-covered ponds, some of the men and boys played a game similar to hockey as early as the 13th century. In this game, players took turns using iron-headed clubs to strike a small ball toward a target, typically a stake or a line marked on the ice. The men would invariably not be shod with skates but would have worn boots with cleats nailed on the soles to avoid slipping over on the ice. Clogs would have been too slippery unless having nails hammered into their soles.

Winter, even in the frigid climate of Holland would eventually give way to spring. Consequently, the thaw would set in and eventually the ponds covering of ice would be freed. Many a Dutchmen or Hollander must have sat there beside his once frozen pond with regret seeing the covering of ice having disappeared.

The game of golf would have been, as it is today, very popular and also habit-forming, so you can imagine the withdrawal symptoms when they could no longer play their game.

It is still a mystery as to how the players would be able to see where they hit their golf balls. One can speculate that they wrapped the ball in a coloured cloth so it would be easily seen in the gloom of a winter's day. The frozen ponds would be crowded with very large Dutchmen or Hollanders hacking away with their golf clubs. If anyone got too close though, then the golf clubs would become a very handy weapon. Historians are very aware of Holland and its colonial aspirations. The national character to take over somebody else's space was commonplace. The sound of golf clubs smacking against thick heads and well-padded bodies would have echoed over the ponds as fights would spring up with little encouragement.

It was a theory that they loathed being kept from playing their favourite sport and one can speculate that it was not long before some golfers adopted the winter game to a summer game. Though in the main the Dutch did not desire blue skies and green fields. The players would rather see their ponds freeze again, as they loved their winter game of golf. They did not have long to wait either as the northern summers are far too short.

Interestingly this is when some two hundred or so years later some visiting Scotsman thought that the summer game had merit. And when he returned home to Scotland he took with him a couple of sets of golf clubs and a supply of golf balls.

In the meantime, other famous Dutchmen were playing golf. Although Rembrandt was not an outdoor type he managed to play every weekend. The great Dutch East India Company also had a great influence on golf and the traders and crew of their ships spread the popular game, in its summer guise, far and wide.

THE SCOTS 1700S

"Golf: A plague invented by the Calvinistic Scots as a punishment for man's sins." – James Barrett Reston

Time has passed since the ancient Romans played a form of golf. Cold and wet Holland had taken up this game and adapted it to their ice-bound ponds during their winter months. Growing tulips was not an option so their new winter sport would have to do.

Any keen Dutch golfer would deftly carve his golf balls from stale gruyere cheese and in no time be out on a frozen pond whacking away. Now, in the highlands of Scotland the clansmen also found that they enjoyed a good game of golf (or as the Scots called it 'goulf') and it soon caught on.

Usually, the favourite pastime of any clansman was cattle rustling. It was also a sport, hobby and a vocation. The Scots just loved the thrill of skulking over the hills to the next valley and lifting the herd of the McWhirters or the McTavishes.

Their second favourite thing to do was to also see if they could steal their neighbour's women. This was not always successful because if they picked the wrong wee lassie they could not always send her back home. She may not have wanted to go home. Finally, a close third in the popularity stakes was a pastime full of mayhem and conflict. It was of course the game of Goulf.

The Kirk had outlawed it but the clansmen knew that what went on in the hills and deep dark valleys was not always known by the Kirk minister.

The boys would set out from their warm beds in their crofts at dawn for a game. They could only afford one golf club and that was made of iron from the village blacksmith who charged them usually one cow or three sheep, as the purchase price.

As you can see only the wealthy, even in those days, could afford to play the game of golf. While doing golf, which consisted of the lads hitting cow turds, they also were always on the lookout for stray cows or lassies. A clansman golfer never rested.

GOLF – THE TRUE STORY

On a bracing day in the Highlands, the lads decided to go and have a game of golf.

The clansmen had one object of the game and that was to see who could hit a cow pat the furthest. For some reason one of the plaid clothed fellows, named Angus, had a knack for the game. Nobody in his village could hit a cowpat as far as he could. He was a real champion and all the boys in the village wanted to be just like him.

The problem with golf was that it could be a dangerous game. The lads had to keep a watchful eye out for any Sassenach or clansman who may lie in wait for them in ambush. You see that while the Scots were out hitting cowpats and stealing cattle and things, the other clansmen and Sassenachs were also doing the same. Consequently, the highlands were always in an uproar.

As a consequence, the fellows would be fully armed along with their golf club. You see as well as hitting cowpats with great gusto there could be more than sore heads for anyone unfortunate enough to stumble upon them.

And speaking of sore heads. They never waited until they reached the nineteenth hole for a drink. The lads would be sipping on their home-distilled 'uisge-beatha', whisky, and by the time it was even too dark for a Scotsman to see his hand in front of his face, let alone hit a cowpat, they were rolling drunk. If it wasn't for their habit of munching on their favourite snack, a cold haggis, which soaked up some of the alcohol, there may have been many more fatalities. It was common in the Highland's game of golf to see drunken Scotsmen left lying on the golf course in a drunken stupor.

It was only when the bagpipes started playing did they rouse themselves and make their way back home. Yes, living in the Highlands could be a grim and harsh life!

Footnote: Did you know this about Scottish Golfers: Do you know why there are 18 holes on a golf course? Because that's how long it took the Scots, who invented the game, to finish their bottle of whisky!

THE ENGLISH 1770S

"Although golf was originally restricted to wealthy, overweight Protestants, today it's open to anybody who owns hideous clothing." – Dave Berry

The aristocracy in England had a lot of leisure time in between fighting each other and the French.

As a consequence, they were always looking around for something to do in their spare time. It was not until one Lord of the realm looked northward to the cold and dark

GOLF – THE TRUE STORY

country called Scotland did a glimmer of an idea come to his dim brain.

He was told that the Scots had been playing a game called golf for some time and it was easy to adapt to the conditions in England. The spacious lands of many wealthy Englishmen were to be the first golf courses for the game. It was a game fit for the aristocracy and no one else though.

Capability Brown was famous, in his day, for designing the aristocracy's gardens and golf courses. How fortunate they were too. The acres of green grass and parklike vistas of the wealthy with their huge mansions, palaces and castles were a perfect place to play the game. The players would have the clubs designed and fashioned by their workmen and the balls and other equipment easily made.

Hit the ball Milord you just teed off with a pork pie.

If any of the poor were desperate enough to poach time on any of the golf courses then they would be severely punished. Some were treated as if they were poachers of deer and were beaten and incarcerated in gaol. Others were locked in the village stocks and forced to endure the discomfort of sitting in an uncomfortable position for days at a time. While locked in the stocks the village people would be encouraged to taunt and treat them cruelly. Rotten fruit, dead dogs and other refuse were all thrown and found their mark. That is why the English are so good at sport, but that is another story.

Other more serious offenders, who repeatedly trespassed on the rolling lawns and glades of the gardens, were arrested, tried in a court of law and later sentenced to be transported to Australia.

When the English learned that the French had been playing the game for some time and were rather good at it the two countries, at first tried a competition of their best teams to meet every year. Regrettably this deteriorated into a trade war and an escalation of arms leading to outright war.

The French by this time had a national sport far more popular than golf and that was called "Bait the English." Mind you the English also had a national pastime called "Give it to the Frogs" and so the two countries attempts at co-existence consisted of periods of war and golf.

In time, though, the English became very good at the game and eventually the French became sick of never winning their golf tournaments. The solution was typically French. They changed the name of golf to "Hit the Ball" and banned any Frenchmen from playing foreigners and only allowed them to play each other.

The English cheered when they learned of this development and rioted roaming the streets and beating up any passer-by who looked French or foreign. The rabble-rousers were easily identified as supporters of their favourite golfer and would wear coloured scarves or hats and even painted their faces to identify with their best players.

The golf players were heroes in the population and all boys wanted to be like them when they grew up. All wanted to be champions at golf and live in big houses in the country and have servants and have cucumber sandwiches and tea with the King.

The English also had a way to ward off the icy northern winds. They would have their caddie serve a pork pie or two with a toddy of rum. Thus cholesterol loaded fat Englishmen, with a pint or two of rum aboard, reeled around the nation's parks and golf courses which was quite a common sight to behold.

THE FRENCH 1770 TO DATE

"A bad attitude is worse than a bad swing." – Payne Stewart

Alright, we know that the French are different! In fact, Bruce has a sneaking suspicion that they want to be. No Frenchman would ever want to be like an Englishman or any other nationality for that matter.

The French are well, er, um, individualists. They too however claim that they invented golf. Or as they call it "Jeu de Golf".

The French historians have long claimed that the origin of golf was in La Belle France. And so we can then assume that for centuries Pierre and his colleagues have hacked away with fervour and flair not emulated by many other golfers. In a major political upheaval, the French had gotten rid of the aristocrats that were hogging all the parks and green fields.

Bruce has ascertained that this is the real reason for the French Revolution and the reign of terror and the busy time for Madame Guillotine.

The aristocrats were sent off in the tumbrils, not for the ill-treatment and neglect of the common man but for the hogging of all the best golf courses.

And another thing, the French always design things differently. You see the golf courses are different in France and even the golf clubs have been designed with a few Gallic idiosyncrasies.

The waiter served red wine and cheese on the 9th hole.

The golf courses were not numbered and had signs displaying the name of the hole. Examples were common such as Cognac the Tough One, Short Calvados or Tricky Absinthe. It was when Count Marcelle d'Burgundy decided to rename all the country's golf courses with famous French battles such as Agincourt Alley, Waterloo Way and Poitiers Place, did the authorities decide to stay with numbers. The good and well-meaning Count, unfortunately, ended up in a tumbril and not a golf cart heading off for an appointment with Madame Guillotine.

Customs and traditions are also different in la belle France. Just imagine a croissant and coffee served by a pretty mademoiselle on the fifth green and on the twelfth a haughty bow-tied waiter in black, waistcoat and white apron offering a player an aperitif with some fromage followed by a glass of red Bordeaux.

The French have style, no doubt about that. It is a lot different in England where you might have a beer and a pork pie with absolutely no chance of anyone resembling a waiter within Cooee. The British don't do things like that, you see.

The golf clubs are all non-conforming, like the French of course, and are shaped differently. In fact, Bruce has designed similar clubs himself.

The golf balls had also been re-designed and were coloured in pastel hues and perfumed with Chanel No 5. One enterprising French designer had fashioned the golf balls out of a type of Gutta Percha (dried sap from the Sapodilla tree) which made the French balls go further than any other nation's.

If anybody has a look at a Citroen DS 21 sedan motorcar, and saw the shape of it, then you would get a pretty good idea of how the Frenchies design their golf equipment. Whether it be their buggies, clothing or clubs.

In later years the rest of the world has caught up. No longer do the French have a monopoly on the game and as everybody else is getting good at it the French are thinking of inventing another game to replace it. In the meantime, the French Government have passed a new law changing the name of the game to 'Taper La Balle' (meaning hit the ball, and that will fall in line with the French policy of avoiding foreign words, like golf, in their vocabulary).

On the golf course, however, the true character of the Gaul shows its ugly head. Exquisite French manners give way to the crowds of French Golfers all wanting to play the same hole at once. The golf clubs are not just used for golf in France. They are a handy weapon as cries of 'Cochon' or 'Chien enrage' are heard, as one golfer tries to putt at the same time as another golfer, on the same putting green and almost coming to blows.

Loud shouts of 'Sacre bleu' or 'Merde' echo around the crowded fairways while the French Players swing wildly at their balls and each other.

'Elan' is a common sentiment in la belle France and the French golfer has it in bucket loads.

THE AMERICANS 1770 TO DATE

> *"Golf is played by twenty million mature American men whose wives think they are out having fun."* –
> Jim Bishop

The American's longing for independence was caused by their desire to be able to play golf where and when they wanted. The British soldiers would confiscate their balls, break their clubs and even fine them but the freedom-loving population were convinced they had right on their side.

The Colonies persevered with their quest for playing golf and had sent Benjamin Franklin as an emissary to England. Franklin happened to be a keen golfer and amongst other diplomatic initiatives, he endeavoured to reason with the stubborn British but with no success. The British were determined to stop the Colonists from playing golf.

A brilliant Home Office clerk came up with a cunning plan which was to impose a tax on all golf equipment imported into the American Colonies. The price of golf equipment became very expensive that the Americans would not buy any and it all came to a head when a shipment of tea and golf equipment docked in Boston Harbour.

Uncle Sam always thought that the wildlife interfered with his golf.

The revolutionary spirit became so strong that a band of supporters of independence disguised themselves as American Indians and forced their way on-board the ship and threw all the tea and golf equipment into the harbour. As you now know war resulted and the British were eventually forced to surrender. The Colonies became the United States of America and started playing golf in real earnest.

The people in America lived close to the wilderness and it was not a rare occurrence to have wildlife wander onto their golf courses. All types of deer, racoons, the shy cougar, alligator and the brown bear, just to name a few. The latter being always difficult to frighten off especially if one was armed with a flimsy golf club. The population, therefore, started carrying some kind of firearm in their golf bag. Which has incidentally led to the large numbers of people bearing arms and the second amendment (The Right to bear Arms).

Over time the Americans became wealthy and a great percentage of the people played golf. The western states were excellent locations for the game and the prairies and grasslands were ideal for long drives. The drives were so long that the people would have wagon trains accompany them to supply food and lodgings and so on.

The native tribes were angry at the crowds of people invading their lands and feared that their favourite games of Lacrosse, scalping the golfers and Bison hunting would die out. The Indian Wars resulted and many golfers were indeed scalped and worse. Many golfers fled from the depredations of the plains Indians and left the huge golf courses on the prairie, to scramble back East to safety.

Over time the Americans invented better equipment, shinier clubs, newer balls and flashier clothes. They even ended up with electric carts to speed around in and some golfers had refrigerators for cold drinks and caddies to carry their golf clubs.

Some Americans even advocated allowing women to play on the golf courses but not permit them to join any golf club. That would come later.

THE AUSTRALIANS 1950S

"Don't play too much golf. Two rounds a day are plenty." – Harry Vardon

Boomerangs thrumming overhead bringing down clouds of flies, while sheep bleating can be heard above the noise of the golfers shouting epithets such as, 'Git orf ya Bugger', 'Stone the bloody crows' and 'fair suck of the sauce bottle'. Yes, the Australian golf courses can be noisy but a lot of fun.

Just about to have a swing, Owen had a funny feeling he was not alone

The Australian golfer in the main is not that well-dressed compared to the French let alone the Americans with their plaid plus-four trousers. Shorts, a T-shirt and a Terry Towelling hat seems to be the norm. The golf carts groan with the supply of beer cans and the weight of Four n' Twenty meat pies. Now you know where the name of the pie originated from.

With mouths dripping with ketchup (tomato sauce) and washed down by a coldie (a beer) of Carlton Draught the Australian golfer is ready for anything.

Unlike his American cousin, the Australian golfer does not have to contend with any stray alligators, but in the North of the country, there are a few potential man-eating crocodiles lurking around, waiting to snaffle a few tasty golfers.

The water buffalo inhabiting the wetter areas of the Northern Territory can add a few extra shots to a game though. As they browse on the succulent grasses of the roughs alongside the fairways, they usually leave great piles of droppings. If one's ball lands in one of these natural hazards then you don't lose a shot, but more fastidious Aussies may prefer to leave the ball where it lies under 20 centimetres or so of crap and lose a shot for a lost ball rather than stir a steaming pile with a handy stick.

Elsewhere crowds of kangaroos look on as the players negotiate the golf links. It does not pay to hook a shot into a mob of roos that's for sure. Getting one's ball back can be fraught and the possibility of being assaulted by a rabid kangaroo is ever on a golfer's mind.

Mobs of emus can also be a problem. Usually, they are shy of the golfers and quickly run off when you approach them. Interestingly, many player blames the giant bird for their

GOLF – THE TRUE STORY

lost balls. Bruce has yet to see an Emu swallow a golf ball but anything is possible on an Australian golf course.

The golf courses in Australia dictate how the game is played. In the wetter parts of the country on the coastal fringe, the courses are usually well laid out and covered in grass. The usual game is played there in between hurried visits to the clubhouse for a top-up or a quick dash behind a tree to relieve one's bladder, as the intake of beer can act as a diuretic. However, further inland where it is much drier, the golfer competes with the Australian wildlife for space on the sparsely covered greens (or browns as they can be called).

The drier areas have golf courses with more dirt than grass: so long shots tend to bounce, or hit a rock, never be seen again. Thus shorter holes with fewer drives are observed.

In the wetter areas, and especially when the annual monsoon period arrives, the courses can be underwater in some patches which can lead to more lost balls. Golfers tend to wear thongs (flip flops) instead of golf shoes and socks so it is relatively easy to discard one's footwear and wade into a puddle and dig around for your ball.

Yes, golf in Australia can be challenging.

2

HISTORY OF THE GOLF BALL

"If you think it is hard meeting new people, try picking up the wrong golf ball." –Jack Lemon

For those who are interested in history as well as golf, the evolution of the golf ball has a very interesting story. This chapter cannot hope to dwell on every type or invented golf ball used by golfers throughout the ages however, some of the main ones are covered here.

Bruce can recall the golf ball having a ball within the cover containing a liquid rubber and also golf balls with metres of rubber band like threads, all designed to give the ball that extra length when hit. Bruce has been heard to mumble, "That the balls may get hit and fly away down the fairway but never straight."

THE LEATHER CLAD STONE OF THE STONE AGE

This projectile was a water-rounded stone, and where necessary the primitive man would round off the stone with abrasion: by rubbing it against a grindstone. Interestingly the archaeologists had misinterpreted these ancient relics and speculated that the stones were used to grind grain, seeds and roots. It has been suggested that these ancient men may have then wrapped the rounded stone within a soft piece of leather.

THE HARD PIECE OF GRUYERE CHEESE ALSO LEATHER WRAPPED OF THE HOLLANDER

The stone used in the ball was in short supply in Holland. Being a lowland with few hills and a few stones. The stone was traded and like the tulip was much sought after. The brilliant idea of moulding gruyere cheese around the flattened stone and then wrapping it in a coloured cloth, showed the genius of the Hollander and Dutchman. The stone was flat like a hockey puck. The problem with using the moulded cheese though were that the rats: they would get at them during the Summer, and then, come Winter, new ones had to be made.

THE COW PAT OF THE SCOTS

No one will ever be able to determine which clansman started hitting cowpats. It is assumed though that the Scots were so poor they could not afford a ball and in their anger, they started hitting cowpats. Mind you they got even angrier if the cowpat was a wet one. Interestingly the Highland cattle were developed solely for the purpose of excreting smaller rounder cowpats. The Scots are ever an intelligent breed and do anything to save a buck.

THE PORK PIE OF THE ENGLISH

Everyone knows that the pork pie can get very hard if not immediately eaten. The English with their pragmatic view of the world soon adopted the rock hard pork pies as an alternative to the golf ball which the French used. Not for the English did they want to use pastel coloured balls or scented for that matter. No, the true Englishman had a tradition to keep up, and the use of the stale pork pies, with their distinctive rotten pork aroma, became a part of history, along with Morris Dancers or Witch burning.

THE PASTEL HUED AND SCENTED GOLF BALL OF THE FRENCH.

Bruce has always been in awe of the French ways of looking at things. Always creative and looking for a better way, called the "French Way". The pastel-hued balls were first painted by Claude Monet in his studio in Giverny and soon all the French golfers wanted to have pastel hued golf balls. Later in 1937, Coco Channel invented the *Channel No 5* perfume, designed to give the golf balls their own unique scent.

THE AMERICANS

Ever the patriotic player, 'The Land of the Free' and so on, the Americans have been known to paint their golf balls with 'Old Glory', their American flag. Teams of inventors and scientists have been slaving away for years to design a better golf ball. Little dimples or big dimples. Small balls, big balls, solid balls and soft-centred balls. All have been manufactured and discarded in the quest for a better American ball.

THE AUSTRALIAN BALL

Australians have been out there inventing things for years. 'Hills Hoists' clotheslines, 'Victa' motor mowers, cardboard boxes for wine and the 'Black Box' for aircraft, but the quest for a better golf ball goes on. The Australian wildlife that inhabits the golf courses are rough on the balls. Consequently, the engineers and inventors are still seeking that important ingredient. A golf ball that goes straight.

There were many other tweaks to the design of the golf balls over the centuries, but some of the more important ones are recorded here.

The ball was initially solid and then moulded from gutta-percha, a form of rubber. Later the balls had a patterned skin to aid the aerodynamics of the flight of the ball. Later a liquid centre was used wrapped with metres of thin rubber bands finally covered by a harder dimpled plastic skin.

Eventually, all this was changed and the golf ball became virtually solid all the way through and had an outer 'skin' of polished dimples.

All that Bruce knows, is that all of the damn things don't go straight!

3

DESIGNING A NEW GOLF BALL

I was recently playing a round of golf with a nice young fellow. On the first hole, which was a long par four with water to the right and a deep ravine to the left, the young man took out a brand new sleeve of balls, teed one up and immediately hit it into the water on the right. Undaunted, he pulled another ball from the sleeve and hit that one into the ravine, as well. Then he took the last ball from the sleeve and hit it, too, into the water. He then reached into his bag and pulled out another brand new sleeve of balls. "Why don't you hit an old ball?" I asked. He responded, "I've never had an old ball."

Sitting there on the couch and watching the pro golf on cable television, Bruce thought he had a brilliant idea that just popped into his mind. He couldn't wait to get down and dirty in his garage where he had his tools and a bench against the rear wall. For the next few hours sounds of whistling, drilling and the word "Eureka" were heard, and then there was silence.

Bruce had been working on a better-designed golf ball. The idea of the current model is that it is supposed to hit the clubface and bounce to wherever the player desires.

The difference with Bruce's new ball was that it was weighted. He theorised that a heavier ball would go further when hit. He had drilled several golf balls and then partially filled them with a core of lead. He was aware that the lead should be centred otherwise the ball's flight would be crooked. Well, more so than his usual attempts.

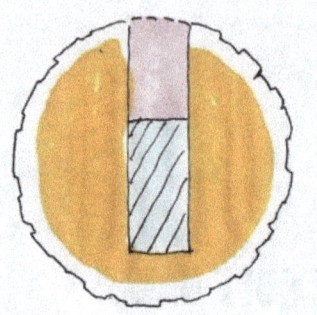

Bruce theorised that a heavier ball with a lead core would go further.

The hole was then filled with epoxy resin and the surface smoothed flush with the surface of the ball.

Another of his brilliant ideas was to glue a hard rubber pad to the clubface to give the ball more bounce.

Bruce could not wait to get out on the course and eventually Sunday dawned and his wife was pleased to get rid of him for the day. He was acting strange, well, stranger than usual, and she was looking forward to some peace and quiet. She could put her feet up, read the New Idea magazine, do the crossword, have some cups of tea and slather some raspberry jam and cream on a few scones. The only problem was that her darling little girl, a cross Poodle, would want to snaffle her scones.

Bruce had a brilliant idea of affixing a hard rubber pad to the clubface.

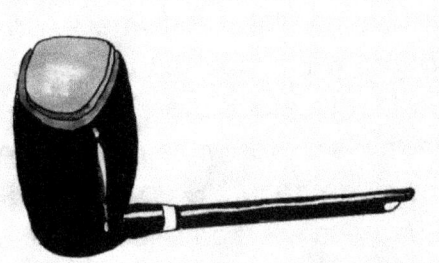

In the meantime, Bruce had met up with his old mate Owen and they drove to the golf course. While during the drive, Bruce did nothing but talk about his new lead-weighted golf ball. Upon arriving at the Clubhouse, Bruce almost ran towards the first tee. Overcoming his usual jitters, Bruce placed his newly designed ball on a tee and proceeded to have a few practice swings. Just to warm-up a bit.

Owen stood there and watched the performance, he was a patient man, but Bruce's antics and verbal diarrhoea were starting to get to him. His natural curiosity had overcome his desire to tell Bruce to just get on with it and he was honest enough to be intrigued to see how Bruce's new ball would perform.

"Now, watch this old boy," crowed Bruce, as with a swing that Babe Ruth would have admired the ball was hit.

Dead silence. Bruce and Owen stood there open-mouthed as the ball cracked into two, with one half winging its way towards the next fairway, and the other just lying there, smirking, showing its belly full of lead and epoxy resin.

"Not to worry mate, said Bruce trying to shrug off his disappointment, I will try another ball and see how that goes."

Owen stood there and uttered not a sound, but his mouth showed the hint of a smile as he observed Bruce's efforts to carry on as if nothing had happened.

OK, here we go mate, and whack, Bruce hit the second ball. It took off and went into orbit as if it was heading for the moon. The two friends stood there in amazement, as the ball disappeared from view over in the next fairway.

Not to be discouraged, Bruce plucked another doctored ball out of the bag and set it on a tee. Not caring to look at the foursome gathered behind him, waiting to tee off.

"Now, you bugger, I want you to take off, straight and true ya hear!" Muttered Bruce through gritted teeth.

Swoosh, crack and then, "yikes, will you look at that mate," exclaimed Bruce, as his ball took off and flew down the fairway, nearly skittling a pink and grey galah which was silly enough to fly across the fairway as Bruce's ball rocketed along.

"Jeez, that went well, but the design could do with a bit of fine-tuning, dontcha think," said Bruce, to a now very grim Owen who, white-faced, was waiting to have his shot, while behind them some grumbling from the second foursome waiting to tee off could be heard.

4

PSYCHOLOGICAL PROFILING

"A leading difficulty with the average player is that he totally misunderstands what is meant by concentration. He may think he is concentrating hard when he is merely worrying." – Bobby Jones

When Bruce was abreast the bar on the nineteenth hole, in between sipping on a few cold beers, he would look around the spacious room and watch all the players gathered there having a drink and carrying on as if they were solving the worries of the world.

It was obvious to him that there was no typical player. Some were enjoying themselves and their laughter echoed around the saloon. Some were sitting quietly looking at their scorecards and appearing down in the dumps while others gazed out the window at the emerald green of the course spread before them. They came in all shapes and sizes too and that was also a continuous source of interest to him.

Bruce had a lot of experience with his fellow man and his time employed as a manager of the Auckland Hotel near

Bondi Beach and later as a real estate agent, which resulted in him being an excellent judge of character. He would often spend his free time just observing the players, to see which category various players would fit into. The following types of golfers are typical of many who haunt the greens worldwide.

THE KAMIKAZE PLAYER

> *"You know what they say about big hitters .... The woods are full of them."* – Jimmy Demaret

This was a player who, in Bruce's opinion, had more courage than brains. This player was brave to the point of foolhardiness. They would typically go for the big shot. A tree in front of them.

"Hell boys, watch this," they would go over it with a sky-climbing hit and scream blue murder when their ball hit a branch and dropped at their feet. They would never learn from this though.

Stuck deep in a sand trap. "Crikey no problem guys," announces our brave fellow.

He would take his wedge and with a mighty swing hit the ball out of the sand trap. Then become amazed when the ball blew at a million miles an hour across the green and ended up resting in the other bunker. Again more screaming and jumping up and down and perhaps a bent and broken sand wedge.

Then comes the next hole, where the ball has to be hit across an expanse of water to the green beyond. It is not far, say 140 metres; an easy shot that requires a wedge or a 9-iron to drop the ball in or adjacent to the hole for a birdie.

The Kamikaze player steps up, plants the ball on his tee with a flourish. Swishes his club like D'Artagnan in the three musketeers and gives the ball the old heave-ho. This player was so positive he was going to cream this hole that he lifted his head before he hit the ball, which then just grazed as the club swished by, hits the ground. Bounces in the air and lands with an audible plop in the middle of the pond. The course echoes with more screaming.

Summary: a brave and mercurial player who enjoyed the thrill and gamble of golf.

THE ANXIOUS PLAYER

> *"Concentration comes out of a combination of confidence and hunger."* – Arnold Palmer

This type of player is well known to all of us and perhaps all of us have been anxious at some time or other. This is the player who has a set routine when about to hit a ball. They know that if they thought about it, they would give up the game altogether and stick to gardening of a weekend. This obsessive compulsion to make sure that each time they have a hit, they follow the same procedure. They place the ball just so. They go through their mental checklist of practice swing, head down, stay calm, keep relaxed, waggle their arse, slow backswing and smooth downswing aiming for that sweet-spot on the club-face.

This is about now when the panic attacks start and halfway through the swing a thought flashes through their mind, that they had forgotten to aim the ball at the flag way in the distance.

After tensing up at the last split second, this player will silently weep tears of blood when the ball does not behave as required and will hop along for 60 metres and hide furtively in the rough.

Is there any wonder then, that the player develops various phobias? They hate a white ball so they get a bright orange box full. They only play of a morning, when it is cooler, and not in the afternoon, when the flies are about. No one in his little group is to talk when teeing off, as any sinner will then have to suffer a dark grimace of suppressed rage.

Summary – Bruce reckons this type of player should learn to relax and enjoy the game but realises that this will never happen.

THE DEPRESSED PLAYER

> *"For this game you need, above all things, to be in a tranquil frame of mind."* – Harry Vardon

This golfer is usually the weekend player and on their good days, they play quite well. This is their manic stage. Laughing and joking the player starts the game with gay abandon. The first nine holes are a dream and he cannot do wrong. The balls are hit with that satisfying click as they soar away, straight and true. Oh, this player just loves the game of golf. He loves his fellow players in his foursome, is enchanted by the greens, the trees and the blue sky. He is on top of the world and looks forward to playing again next week.

On the tenth teeing off though, something happens to make the player's mood change, like a switch was thrown. The ball is there sitting proudly on a long wooden tee and the Number 1 Wood is poised to send it unerringly on its way towards the flag fluttering in the distance, some 350 meters away. Crack goes the clubhead and the ball soars away over

GOLF – THE TRUE STORY

the trees into the next fairway. Suddenly the player is in a rage. This game of golf is a bastard of a game. He hates it with a venom. Nothing goes right for him as he stomps down the fairways over the next nine holes. He loathes his fellow players. Can't stand the sight of them. Seethes with rage at the trees having the temerity to sway in the wind and curses the cloudless blue sky thus enabling the sun to blaze down and no doubt giving him a dose of sunstroke or at worst, skin cancer.

Summary: This player should remember to take their pills and perhaps try another game like ten pin bowling.

EATING DISORDERS.

Our next player is the adored husband of a good cook. His mates settle for a meat pie and tomato sauce at the tuck shop, but not this guy. His beloved missus has packed a gourmet meal for him. Already nudging 112 kilos, our hungry golfer always looks forward to his meal break. He sits down on a handy bench. He then places a linen serviette beside him and on his plate of bone china, tears off the glad wrap and falls upon the meal. With a gnashing of teeth and a few grunts and smack of his lips the food disappears. His small bottle of wine is opened and two glasses of Pinot Noir are glugged down. Later, he is ready to resume the game. His lady wife has also supplied him with some snacks, which he munches lustily as he trudges gamely down the next fairway.

His fellow players almost look forward to seeing this display of gluttony, as much as playing the game and marvel at their friend's ability to function, let alone play the game.

Summary: In no time this hungry fellow finds that he is looking forward to getting back to the clubhouse and having a few cold beers and some potato chips. The salt will be an excellent replacement for salt lost whilst he has been sweating his way around the eighteen holes.

PERSONALITY DISORDER TYPE

"If you wish to hide your character, do not play golf." – Percey Boomer

This player, whether male or female, may find that golf brings out their worst behaviour. The stress of the game, the desire to succeed or do well, all bring forth the most negative feelings.

One particular red flag to this bull is the group of players meandering down the course in front of them. He or she is in a hurry, fervently demanding the right of way, and when the laughing foursome all lose their balls and start thrashing around in the rough, this player begins to seethe.

In no time, shouting starts and the offending players good-naturedly invite him to play through.

The player on the next fairway slices his ball, which ends up on the fairway in front of our very angry and pugnacious friend. He again starts shouting and with much waving of his arms and tells the hapless fellow to just wait as he has the right of way.

Bad manners, rages, kicking balls and general misbehaviour seems to be the symptoms of this angry boorish player. They are just not fun to play with and eventually players avoid them like the plague. Bruce has long speculated, that the boxing academies and Karate Dojos may be full of short-tempered and aggressive ex-golfers who have abandoned the game.

Summary: The game of golf is something to enjoy and not take too seriously unless you are a professional and your income depends on excellence. If this player finds the game so fraught and is so miserable then it is suggested they take up some other kind of pursuit like martial arts.

POST-TRAUMATIC STRESS

> *"It's how you deal with failure that determines how you achieve success."* – David Feherty

This condition usually affects golfers when they are about to tee off. Just watch, the next time you are waiting on the first tee for your turn to play and watch the other players all lined up.

There is always one golfer who hates an audience. You can see it, for when it is his turn, he has 'the hunted look,' nervously looking around, wishing he were somewhere else, anywhere else. For you see everyone is watching him. Thousands of eyes all staring at him. Watching his every move. Waiting for him to miss-hit.

Now that may not be the case, but he thinks they are. He is so busy praying not to make an ass of himself that he tightens up and instead of hitting the ball his usual 180 metres or so, it gives out a dull clunk and then skims the grass for 40 metres.

His shoulders are slumped, as he knows he just cannot take a Mulligan in front of all those people. He collects his tee, slams his driver back in the bag and grabs the handle of the buggy to trudge off down the fairway. He knows that his performance will be remembered forever-more by all of the players. Henceforth, he will always have that nagging suspicion that every time he goes to tee off in front of people, he will again have the same result.

Summary: The cure for this condition is to have a few drinks before one goes out to play, that may do the trick.

THE POSITIVE THINKER

> *"I'm the best. I just haven't played yet."* – Muhammed Ali

We have all played with this type of golfer. Infuriating, isn't he? They can concentrate and they are very serious. They can sometimes give you tips, which you invariably cannot seem to make work.

FINAL NOTE

Our Bruce is one of those amateur psychologists as you can see from this chapter 'Psychology Profiling", though you may agree with him on some of these points raised. Who hasn't thought that their fellow player may suffer from some kind of neurosis or psychosis? Editor's note: many golfers are deluded anyway, to think they can hit that silly ball straight.

5

THE EQUIPMENT

"Golf is a game whose aim is to hit a very small ball into an even smaller hole, with weapons singularly ill-designed for the purpose." – Winston S. Churchill

Mr Churchill was a man who knew a lot about weapons and their design, so his few words, seen above, came close to one of the main problems with the game of golf. The poorly designed equipment.

To play golf an aspiring player must have a full kit of clubs plus a few other items that will make their entry into the game of kings, one of pleasure with a few moments of frustration along the way.

The Hacker, like our hero Bruce on a bad day, usually uses his trusty 7-iron and putter and he is quite content to play the 18 holes with these two clubs. However, as his mate Gazza said, "You will never get any better, playing the way you do." And alas, he was correct.

Other golfers of course use all the clubs, not necessarily all at once. The very large wood, which Bruce calls a 'Boomer' for the drives. Hybrid woods for median fairways and then the irons, ranging from the number 2 or 3 iron to the 9-iron. All clubs are supposed to hit a ball set distances, so it is recommended you go to a golf range and make note of how far you hit the ball with each club.

Bruce tried this once and most of the balls went about the same distance, so in his case, he had to go back to have another course of lessons from the pro.

Choosing the right gear can be confusing.

Then you have the wedges for those short shots up and onto the putting greens. The Wedge and then the sand wedge, the latter supposed to get you out of any bunker you are unfortunate enough to dribble into.

A handy club is the Chipper and this is used like a Putter but has a clubhead that is angled and so your ball will then gracefully arc away and land either in the cup or beside the flag. Well, that's the idea anyway.

THE FULL KIT AND CABOODLE

Before we get into all the serious bits, let's make sure we have a full kit before we start.

Having all the clubs doesn't end there. You will need a buggy with large balloon tires and a seat, as those eighteen holes seem to be getting longer and longer nowadays. The balloon tires are to make it easier to pull or push the gear around the course and also to leave no tracks in the lush green grasses.

The seat attached to your buggy is invaluable in Bruce's opinion. It is a place to put your lunch, a cold beer or drink when you stop for a break. The seat is handy if you become weary, just taking the weight off your feet for the time that your golfing partners putt or tee off, gives you a welcome few minutes to recharge the batteries.

Most golf bags have two loops for an umbrella and also capacious pockets to store a supply of golf balls, jacket, sunscreen, personal items, spare pencils and a large ring to thread your hand towel through. There are usually smaller loops for the collection of tees that you require.

Bruce, and a few other people he knows who play golf, are full of aches and pains after they play a round. So they take a couple of painkillers a half-hour before the game, washing them down with plenty of water. *That seemed to do the trick!*

The hot days in Australia make it so necessary to hydrate as much as possible. The only problem is that when you are out on the ninth hole, for example, and you hit your ball into the trees, you end up using the trees for another purpose.

There are other items you will need too. The Ball Retriever used to retrieve balls in water hazards. Some of Bruce's experimental clubs, personal insect protector spray, sunscreen tube or bottle, cap or hat.

Other items you may need are: an axe or a small hatchet, for clearing your ball's path; or secateurs, to trim any bush that gets in the way. Bruce usually carries birdseed or kangaroo feed for the wildlife and spends a good deal of his time observing nature. This occupation usually breaks his concentration and his golf game deteriorates. That is his excuse anyway.

Even a small shovel can come in handy, as some of the courses Bruce plays on out in the bush can be pretty rough. A billiard cue for those experimental putts.

Conversely instead of something to attract the wildlife Bruce carries a homemade catapult (British) or as some of his mates call it a Shanghai (Australian). This is for the crows that can inhabit the course or the rabbits that dig up the greens.

GOLF – THE TRUE STORY

Room for a couple of Bruce's radically designed clubs, the bat-like club for those long shots down the fairway and of course the long tee.

Hey, how many times have you played a game of golf as someone's guest and you are a new chum to the course? Thankfully some golf links have scorecards with a schematic plan showing dog legs and such on each hole.

"Caddy, why do you keep looking at your watch?" asked the curious golfer." It's not a watch, sir. It's a compass"

THE CADDIE

A professional or a talented amateur may also employ a caddie. These are golfers who expect to be paid to lead you around the course and suggest the best way to play your shot.

The question is, are the caddies always right with their advice?

Bruce always says that, 'Caddies know a heck of a lot more than I would, and that's for sure.' Although it would never be a factor for his game or most of the other players either, to have the luxury of a caddie.

GOLF BALLS

Also required are a dozen golf balls, preferably coloured, so you can see where the damn things have been hit. Mind you Bruce takes as many balls as he can, just in case he has a bad day and loses a swag of them.

You will need white balls for autumn though as the orange and yellow balls are lost in the leaves dropping, for those colours are excellent camouflage.

Then in summer, you can go back to using the coloured balls as they show up on the green of the fairways.

Years ago, Bruce was driving through the countryside, way out west in the red soil country. He passed a golf course that had no grass on it at all. What made it interesting though, was that the red baked ground was littered with pieces of sparkling white quartz. It has always been his dream to play on that course and to first paint all his golf balls a bright green.

TEES

A player will need tees to tee off on. Bruce initially just went along with the coloured plastic ones and eventually realised that he was prone to digging in too deep with his shot. In fact, sometimes, he dug so deep that he almost dislocated his wrist when the clubhead came to a sudden stop.

No divot will lift gracefully in the path of your ball as it speeds away, straight as a die, towards the flag in the distance. No, you will find that your ball has dribbled along the ground and sits there smirking away as you massage your wrists and then search the face of your club to see if it is still the right way around.

Mind you many of the courses in Australia were so rough and dry that any hit of the clubhead on the ground would result in a broken club or worse. The tees would not even go into the ground it is so hard, so a preferred lie is usually the local rule.

The problem was solved when an American pal gifted Bruce a packet of some very long wooden tees. These are about 7 centimetres in length and the ball rests quite high. The result is that Bruce now avoids his usual digging up of the ground when he hits the ball.

SCORECARD AND AN ERASER

"I have a tip that can take five strokes off anyone's game: It's called an eraser." – Arnold Palmer

Bruce always enjoys visiting different golf courses and used to collect the scorecards. Some are most attractive and have coloured covers, others have maps of the course. The scorecard is usually made available to a player when they purchase the game at the clubhouse. During the game, many a scorecard has been 'edited' and an eraser (or *rubber* as it is called in some parts of the world) is always helpful.

THE BALL RETRIEVER

This useful aid to one's golf bag is designed to retrieve balls that end up in the water. Whether it be in the ponds or creeks or even large puddles, this item can be most helpful, especially if you want to avoid getting wet feet.

THE HATCHET

A short-handled axe can be of use to the golfer. Let me explain. Ending up in the rough behind a tree with a branch in the way of your swing can be a real problem. However, perhaps while your partner off helping you look for the ball, you could whip out the axe, hack off the offending branch, and stow the axe again before he is any the wiser. But if he happens to ask, 'What was that noise?' you could always blame it on a woodpecker or something.

SECATEURS

Now, that pesky tree or shrub that gets in the way can be easily dealt with by the use of this handy tool. Nicely new and sharp secateurs are ideal for cutting back any offending branches that obscure the view of the fairway.

THE SHOVEL

Not for all the tall stories, but to dig your way out of the rough or bunker.

Note: only use this when you are out of sight, and with practice you can be quick about it.

SUNTAN BLOCK

Playing golf in summer in Australia can give you a good dose of sunstroke or at worse third-degree burns from the sun.

Recommendation: Suntan lotion a long sleeve shirt and a hat.

INSECT SPRAY

During the day, flies, millions of the buggers. In some parts of Australia, especially the sheep country, you are plagued with the things. They pack onto your back, and with every twitch they head for anything with moisture. Lips, eyes, brow and yes, your mouth. In the cool of the day when you are close to finishing up, the flies head for the hills and the mosquitoes take over.

Recommendation: that you have a good personal insect spray of some kind and remember to keep your mouth closed.

COOL DRINK CONTAINER

Yes, it can get hot in the 'Land of Oz' and if you are reading this book in America or Britain, well it can get hot there too.

The answer is to stay hydrated. A thermos or insulated drink vessel is excellent and should keep cool when you are out there getting blasted by the sun.

Recommendation: don't put alcohol in the container. Your game may suffer.

PAIN KILLERS

The old body isn't as good as it used to be. Bruce has a mate called Owen, who had an interesting way of overcoming any aches and pains as the result of giving his body beautiful a work out playing golf. He always takes a couple of painkillers before a game. By this means, he avoids the backache that he is plagued with.

Recommendation: if you are over 65, now may be the time to take heed. The pills are far better than a couple of nips of scotch. You may never get out of the bar to play your game, if you rely on a scotch to help. Mind you it is best to have drinkies after playing than before.

GOLF GLOVE

Well, Bruce is not sure if this helps, but he is keen to try anything to improve his handicap. The golf glove is supposedly used to stop the formation of blisters and callouses and slipping. Regrettably, the best gloves in the world will not help our Bruce, but you can wear one of these and see if it helps you.

Recommendation: Bruce's favourite colour is blue.

DIVOT FORK

Ever seen one of these? Well, they are available at your pro shop or any golf equipment retailer. Bruce has always been impressed by his mates who hit a ball cleanly and see it lob onto the green near the flag, but see a great big dent in the smooth green lawn. Of course the players, dutifully work the ball mark with the fork until it virtually disappears. This will, therefore, ensure a smooth putting surface and make it easier for other players to putt with no mishaps.

Recommendation: make an effort and help the greenkeeper and your fellow players. You may help them, but it will not do much good for poor old Bruce.

THE GOLF CART AND BUGGY

Now, buggies, these are important because you do not want to be carrying your bag of clubs and other equipment over the long distances of eighteen holes. Bruce simply loves the electric golf cart. One problem though is that he enjoys it so much it breaks his concentration a trifle. Speed on these carts is dampened to a measly ten or so kilometres an hour but accidents can occur. Going sideways up a rise or speeding along to get a run on at that hill, when a bunker may be lurking in wait can lead to disastrous consequences. So watch out for those bunkers!

Bruce tended to go too fast when driving.

The manual buggy is easy to use and inexpensive. However, having a seat on it is the way to go. The seat is a handy place to rest your tired old body and give you that extra energy to breast the bar on the nineteenth hole.

There are a few of the champions at the Club, who use a buggy that has a battery-operated motor and that is handy for those hills and over the long distances of those 400-metre fairways.

6

DESIGNING ALTERNATE GOLF GEAR

"I don't let birdies and pars get in the way of having a good time." – Angelo Spagnolo

That word non-conforming rears its ugly head here in this chapter. Bruce has sat there on his comfortable couch for years and has dreamed about golf, imagining how he would play a shot and of course congratulated himself on winning again. In his daydreams that is.

Bruce can recall, way back in the 1970's, Sydney had a popular and famous Lord Mayor called Leo Port. Now, Leo was a clever guy. Not only was he a talented politician, but was also a very practical engineer.

One of his many talents was as a panellist on the ABC show called the Inventors. Bruce remembers one show, where Leo was talking about the antiquated way in which golf clubs are designed. He reasoned that as an engineer he could design new golf clubs that would be far superior to those currently used.

Consequently, Bruce has taken him at his word. Although he is not an engineer he is somebody, who besides being a professional couch potato, always looks for the easy way. This chapter on "Designing Alternate Golf Gear", warrants scrutiny.

Before we start, let's make sure we all are aware of what golf clubheads can be made from. Usually, they are made from Aluminium and zinc alloys which are found in golf club sets for beginners. Other materials such as HST Aluminium, which is much harder than ordinary aluminium, is more popular in large drivers. A form of stainless steel is found in the iron heads that professionals use.

THE SWEET-SPOT

Another important feature in the design of the modern golf club is to have a larger sweet-spot. If you have ever played tennis, for example, then you would already be familiar with the feel and sound the racquet makes "ping" when you hit the ball dead centre, so too with the golf club. That is why you are seeing larger and larger golf clubheads, where the sweet-spot is bigger. It gives less cause of error.

The big woods are now as large as soup bowls and with the hollow metal heads, the ball definitely has the sound of a "ping" as it speeds on its way. As a consequence, Bruce has therefore had a stab at various golf club designs, to firstly have a bigger sweet-spot and secondly to hit the ball easier and further.

THE FLEXIBLE SHAFTED DRIVER OR CLUB

Another theory of Bruce's is to have a slightly flexible shaft on a club. The idea is to increase the speed of the clubhead and save one's ageing back. The flexible section of the shaft, would create a whip-like action to the clubhead and therefore increase the velocity of the clubface meeting the ball. Thus resulting in a ball going faster and further and hopefully straighter.

Oddly the concept of a flexible shafted club is not a new one. The game of 'Hornussen', in Switzerland, uses a flexible driver, called a pole, and can be from 2 to 3 metres in length. It then hits the ball, a 'Hornuss', which speeds away at a velocity of 300 kms per hour and travels up to 400 metres or more.

THE LONG TEE AND DRIVER

If you have watched a cricketer or baseball player, you will observe that the batsman does not always have to lean over and contort himself into a pretzel to have a swing at the ball.

Bruce's creative mind has now come up with a solution to all this. He reasoned that a new driver, shaped like a cricket bat and swung like a baseball bat, may be a lot easier than what golfers are expected to do by the professionals.

If this were to take place, then a cricket bat shaped club would need to be designed and a long flexible tee used to bring the ball up to say waist level to enable a swing at the ball.

THE CRICKET BAT CLUB

This club, see illustration below, has been fashioned from a piece of board and cut and sanded to the shape required. The face of the "bat-like club" has had a thin sheet of rubber glued. The swing is virtually horizontal to the ground and it enables those desk-bound golfers with bad backs to take a hefty swing with fewer aches and pains.

THE LONG TEE

The usual tees available for golf are from 1.5 to 4 inches in length and Bruce has a whole collection of them. Not that he is mean, but he does so enjoy collecting all the unbroken tees laying around. (And balls for that matter.)

The tee that Bruce has designed, is a rather lengthy effort. To enable the new club's cricket or baseball swing, without bending that stiff old back, the ball needs to be 90 cms from the ground. The head of the tee also has to be unbreakable, so it has been made from rubber.

The lacrosse stick with its attached net may also be of interest in lofting your ball further than you normally do. The physics here is similar to the use of an atlatl or spear thrower, these two devices increase the speed of the spear and also make it travel further.

GOLF – THE TRUE STORY

Owen cooly prepared to have a swing with the newfangled bat.

BALL LAUNCHER

If anyone has been at a dog park and seen owners of large dogs trying to throw a ball for their pal, will see the ball not travel too far, and the efforts of their owners are not appreciated as the dog is not getting much of a workout. However, for those owners who have for example border collies, who love to run, and will run all day, they use a ball thrower.

Now, this same principle may be a nice way to get that golf ball to go further. Naturally the longer the ball thrower the further the ball goes.

THE NEW PUTTER

Putting! Blimey. Who was the imbecile that thought up this crazy way of hitting a ball? Well, whoever it was they must have been a halfwit, or sadist, I cannot decide.

Just remember where you were at the weekend. Right on the edge of the green where you arrived after two great shots, what a beauty!

There you are 15 metres away from the green and the coast looks clear. You have seen the experts hunker down on their haunches to read the green you see. So you do that and for the life of you, it doesn't look so different down there as it did when you were standing up.

Never mind, you did see though that there was a bit of a lump in the green halfway to the cup and the green sort of slants from left to right.

Okay, that looks easy, so you are in a hurry and have no idea how to handle it anyway. Ignore all that and just go for it. Hit the damn ball right in the guts and get as close as you can to the flag and then one more putt and you're down in four. Whacko!

Now, four putts later, you are staring at a six, a double bogie and perhaps another putt to put the blasted ball away. What a disaster.

Anyhow, just imagine if you could get an average of two putts per hole? Just what would that mean to your handicap?

So you can see the importance of good putting. Bruce may have some answers here that will help you achieve your dream. He has designed some new types of gear.

THE CROQUET TYPE PUTTER

Have you ever wondered why the founding fathers of the game of golf designed clubs to be played at the right angle of your body? What with all the parallax error and the uneven surface of the putting green, makes putting virtually impossible to excel at for the amateur golfer.

Bruce has often struggled with this part of the game and would welcome easy ways to overcome the four putt per hole game that he usually plays.

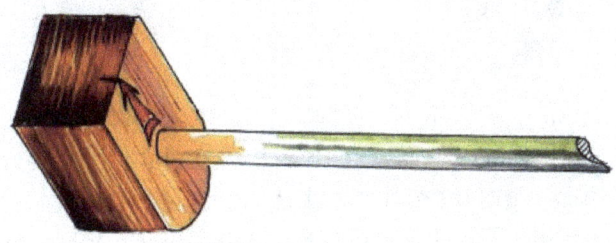

In the meantime, he has come up with a design of a putter to do away with the problems as described above. He has designed a putter shaped more like a croquet mallet, rather than a golf putter. The action required to play the shot is to stand behind the club and have it swing backwards and forwards, just like in croquet.

Alright, I hear you say, "That is non-conforming" however, Bruce and his mates are not playing to be champions or to scramble to reduce their handicap. They are in the game for that three-letter word called, "F.U.N."

NEW PUTTER AND DRIVER WITH SPRING PLATE HEAD

Another one of Bruce's inventions was the spring-loaded mallet type head. A wood in the true sense this strange-looking club was fashioned from a heavy block of wood. A spring was affixed to the block and a plate with a rubber pad was then riveted to the spring.

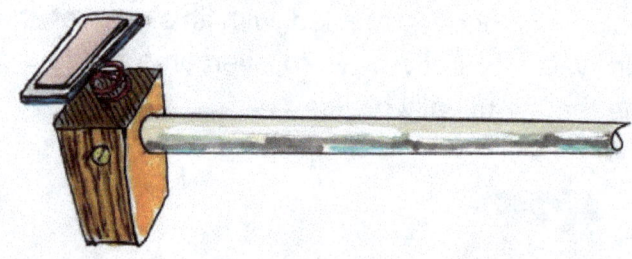

The intention was to use the weight of the clubhead and then the high tensile steel spring's energy to hit the ball and gain length. The theory is that little swing takes place and so there is less cause for hitting the ball crooked.

THE PENDULUM PUTTING AID

This contraption, at the date of writing this book, is still in the design process. The idea is to have a tripod that can enable the ball to be hit with no tremor or deviation by the player. The theory is to hit the ball in or as near as possible to the hole and this pendulum-type-aid, again non-conforming, may be a lot of fun.

THE BROOM HANDLE PUTTER

Yep, Bruce has always been interested in that thing. He didn't design this piece of sadism, but it rates a mention. A long handle say 4 metres or a good 30 centimetres or more-longer than a normal sized putter. Alas, there are a whole lot of rules for and against this "Belly Putter" and Bruce has avoided buying one. Not because it is legal or illegal, it is just too expensive. The poor lad is not broke but he is careful with his money, or really the memsahib is, and Bruce is scared of her. Anyone who is having a dose of the horrors with their putting, should consider trying one of these things.

THE LASER SIGHT AND ACCESSORIES

Have you ever seen those laser torches (or flashlights), they are sure a lot of fun. Bruce has thought about the use of one of these affixed to the putter's shaft and used to point the way for the swing and ball towards the cup.

It is a helpful way of aiming and it is a wonder that nobody else has thought of it. Just don't shine the damn thing at any passing aircraft. Otherwise, the gendarmes will give you a free holiday in Long Bay jail.

THE SWATTER

The new swatter is now born, so throw away your putter and don't bother to invest in a broomstick putter either, because there is a new design of a club that is handy for you and is bound to work.

It seems that it would be a very good idea to adopt the stance of a croquet mallet and this will give your ball a straighter path to the cup.

If you persist in using your current putter, it may be a good idea to affix a swivel of some kind. The laser light can then be inserted and then with the aid of the butterfly screws, moved up or down so as to shine the laser in the direction you wish the ball to go. Thus, you can use as your sighting mechanism to make sure that you were heading in the right direction towards the cup.

THE FLORSHEIM WEDGE - SHOE ATTACHMENT

Otherwise known as the Florsheim Plate - Another handy invention by Bruce is the 'Florsheim Wedge' which can be easily affixed to the toe of your right boot if you're right-handed, or left as the case may be. Thus this handy golf aid can be used when you inadvertently end up in a bunker. You see, if your sand wedge shots are starting to mount up and you want that pesky ball to get out of that bunker then this simple device will come into its own.

This handy aid to Bruce's game, was discovered when he was laying on his couch daydreaming. Suddenly it came to him. Why rely on the edge or toe of your shoe and see the ball skid off at an angle from where you want it to go.

Without delay he hastened to the garage, where he kept his tools, remembering to take with him a tube of super glue. In no time he had cut out a small section of three-ply and sanded it. A small wedge to give the plate the right degree of lift was then glued to the plate. The plate was then affixed carefully to his right golf shoe.

Note: It may be a good idea to use this, when your partner or fellow players are looking the other way.

Remember when you affix the plate to your shoe to make sure it has a degree of lift, so your ball will rise gracefully and end up hopefully near the pin.

Note: remember to paint the Florsheim Wedge, as Bruce calls it, the same colour as the shoe; for camouflage you see.

ENORMOUS GRIPS

Obviously, Michael Jordan the famous basketball player, with a height of 6' 5" (almost 196 cms) also has huge hands, evidenced by the ease of which he palms an NBA-sized basketball. As such, he has huge grips on his clubs. Jordan was arguably the greatest basketball player ever, but he's also no slouch on the golf course either. His "Airness" is a 1.2 handicap. Mr. Jordan also owns a 3,500 sq ft putting green which he had installed in his own backyard. He averages 36 holes a day.

Bruce can't say, but attention to the grips on your clubs may be more important than once thought. There are a host of aids such as grip tape that can be used. Have a good look around at all this sort of thing and experiment.

7

THE GOLF SWINGS

"You swing your best when you have the fewest things to think about." – Bobby Jones

THE SWING

Possibly one of the hardest things to do while playing golf is to have a perfect golf swing. For some unaccountable reason, some of us are naturals, while we mere mortals struggle. There is no easy way to have a perfect swing, as most adapt to what is comfortable for them.

Once Bruce had the pleasure of playing a game of golf at Bathurst NSW, and the three other fellows with him were considering who was going to be playing with whom. He had a good long look at his fellow golfers and saw that one was grossly overweight and to make matters easier for him to select his partner, the portly fellow had a most peculiar golf swing. It was a very fast whip around type of thing. A sort of a forehand at tennis versus a cricket bat hit to the boundary swing. The intrepid Bruce has reasoned that it was bound to be a fizzer.

It was thus, easy for Bruce to choose another one of his companions, as he had judged the other fellow to be of no value as a player at all. In fact, Bruce thought he was rather clever being so analytical and congratulated himself on his choice.

The important thing is to relax and concentrate.

Well, imagine Bruce's surprise when he saw that the fellow's weird style of play, resulted in drives close on 300 metres and straight too. The other parts of his game were equally as surprising and had excellent results.

By the eighteenth hole, Bruce's opposition had won the game and beat Bruce and his partner by a mile and it also convinced Bruce, to abandon the disciplines thrust upon him by the Club's resident pro. He would forevermore, just be comfortable and do the best he could.

Bruce also realised, with a sinking heart, that if a player is going to be either a champion or a hacker it depended on your genes or the 'God of Golf'.

HOW LONG SHOULD YOU TAKE?

Bruce is always conscious of taking too much time, as he well knows how irritated he can get with other players who head down, talking to themselves and going through various checklists seem to stand there in a contorted pose forever trying to get in the groove.

He had been told by the pro to have his hands on the club grip a certain way. This was all Latin to Bruce as he could never remember where to put his fingers and eventually just grabbed the handle and hoped for the best.

Then the lead up to teeing off, head down, waggle your hips, think positive, visualise where the ball is to go and above all, relax. Hold the club firmly but not too hard. Ignore your golf partner's possible inadvertent breaking of wind, cough or sneeze or any other ploy to put him off his game. Try and keep his mind blank and concentrate on the game. And alas failing in a big way, as inadvertently the thought pops into his mind that he would have to cut the lawn when he gets home.

He had to then get rid of this thought of mowing and remember to visualise how he hits and swings and sends the ball on its way. Just like the pro has been coaching him. And so the points in Bruce's mental checklist is slowly being checked off while his other mates patiently wait until he finishes.

Suddenly, a voice broke into his consciousness.

"Oye, hurry up Brucie, we can't spend all day!"

With a start, Bruce breaks his concentration and fumes as he casts a look of daggers at the impatient ex-friend. Despite the fellow looking ostentatiously at his watch, Bruce doggedly starts laboriously going through his mental checklist all over again.

Painful isn't it?

Now, the swing is not just confined to the drives. It is of paramount importance to have a perfect swing when using the irons. Bruce can vouch for this as many of the golf links that he plays on are not up to the standard of the ones where the professionals play. Bumpy fairways with slopes that feed his ball into the rough or even worse into the pond, you name it.

He once played a game up at a golf course in Nelson Bay (NSW) many years ago and the whole course seemed to be built in a swamp. Beside every green and fairway, was a mire of mud and water with thick weed and sedges. If he hit a ball, any ball, then the damned thing would roll and end up in the drink. He found that his irons let him down that day and despite borrowing some balls from his mates, he still ended the day with no balls remaining, a raging thirst for a cool beer and a vow never to play on that course again. Unless he learned how to hit a ball better.

Now we come to the swing with the wedge and the sand wedge. Again, another mystery to Bruce as to how to use this thing better. Some days he can hit with these clubs like a dream. Although his putting stinks and his drives go every which way as he tacks to and fro up and down the fairways.

The sweet-spot is so very important with a wedge. There you are standing there so pleased with your effort to get this far with two shots. Thoughts of a wedge shot and a one putt fill your head, as you achieve a very rare par for the hole.

Don't forget to keep your head down now! The cup is only 20 metres away and a wedge should lift your ball nicely and drop close to the cup and then roll a little. You draw back your club remembering to do it slowly and then bring the clubhead down smoothly to kiss the ball and send it on its way.

Crack the rim of the clubface hits the ball and send it 40 metres away over the putting green and ends up sitting there smugly sparkling white in the sun, 20 metres from the cup on the other side of the green.

Yes, the swing is so important, but the game of golf is a cow.

And now we come to the swing required for the putt. When Bruce watches the Pro Golf and sees the professionals play, he like millions of other viewers, marvel at their putting. It is uncanny as to how they can smoothly draw back their putter and send the ball on its merry way unerringly towards the cup and then vanish from sight. Ah, that looked easy, didn't it.

The swing is important let's face it, but the game of golf is not easy for the weekend Hackers. It is character-building stuff though.

THE CORRECT GRIP

As Sam Snead was oft to say, "If a lot of people gripped a knife and fork the way they do a golf club, they'd starve to death."

Imagine when you are asked to put the cat out by the good wife, how you would hold the cat. Right? Well, wrong.

That has nothing to do with it. Holding the golf club is an art and for anyone with a touch of arthritis, it can be uncomfortable. Therefore, grab the stick with a reasonably hard grip and hope for the best. That is what Bruce does anyway.

KEEP YOUR HEAD DOWN

Bruce was given a tip by the Club's pro when he was browsing in the Pro Shop.

Chuck suggested that Bruce should keep his head down when hitting the ball. You see Bruce had fallen into some bad habits that were glaringly obvious to the professional golfer.

The reason why our hero lifted his head was that he was always eager to see how his ball would swoop up and then gracefully arc down and bounce a few times and hopefully come to rest in the middle of the fairway. That is his fairway and not the one next door.

The pro reckoned that this was the reason why he was not hitting the ball cleanly, as that split second of lifting his head resulted in his club moving just a touch.

Bruce was therefore eager, to try out this gem of information about the shortcoming of his game.

There he was twisted into impossible knots following the pro's advice how to tee off and he determinedly kept his head down. Not for Bruce would he wander from any good advice. No way!

Crack went the ball, as it was hit by Bruce's driver and away it sped. Never to be seen again.

You see Bruce had his head down and couldn't see where the damn thing had gone.

When he asked his mates, "Didja see where it went fellas," the answer was in the negative, as they were not paying attention. What great pals.

THE STANCE

"No matter how good your get, you can always get better – and that's the exciting part." – Tiger Woods

GOLF – THE TRUE STORY

The Golf Pro always teaches you to address the ball. This does not mean that you say, "Gidday, how are you?" or anything like that.

What these superior beings preach, is that you stand there in a contorted position so you can hit the ball cleanly. This uncomfortable stance would send any chiropractor into raptures, as a host of new patients will be heading his or her way.

The many and varied instructions are like this. Look down and keep your eye on the ball, legs astride and pointing where the ball is to go, head down and don't look up, bum loose, arms in a certain way, (Bruce can never remember which way that is). The pro's instructions finish up with the final and painful advice, grasp the golf club with your fingers contorted thus, so your arthritic joints scream in anguish.

Slowly bring your club back, until your body would give a contortionist a nervous breakdown and then smartly and smoothly swing and of course follow through, remembering to hit the ball and not the ground. Comfortable? We would defy you to hit the ball with any confidence. Oh, yes, and then remember to look up and see where your ball has ended up.

Bruce has never mastered all this and has fallen into bad habits. He just does the best he can and let's fly. Being a spiritual person (well, kind of) Bruce also quietly says a little prayer.

THE PUTT

"A shot that goes in the cup is pure luck, but a shot to within two feet of the flag is skill." – Ben Hogan

The putter is probably the most difficult club to use in your bag. Just imagine, if you could reduce the average number of putts by one per hole. That would improve your final score by 18! The mind boggles.

Next weekend Bruce is out and about on his favourite course at Royal Turramurra on Sydney's north shore. The first hole is an easy one and he is on the green, which is quite nicely maintained. Unlike some links that Bruce has played on, the green surface is not pockmarked with dents from other golfer's efforts.

Bruce always admired the golfers who got down there to see where the bumps were.

His ball has come to rest just a short way from the cup and it should be an easy two putt for Bruce, and a one putt for many other golfers. He remembers how the professionals do it and brings his putter back smoothly, then like a pendulum, it scythes back to hit the ball and send it on its way. It rolls along happily and stops 15 centimetres from the cup.

No problem, Bruce straddles the ball, tenses up, this is looking easy, starts sweating, imagines that everybody is looking at him, starts counting the shots that have got him this far. Then looks at the grass and thinks how nice it looks and then hits the ball, which then miraculously sails past the cup and ends up 30 centimetres on the other side.

THE MULLIGAN

"Mulligan: invented by an Irishman who wanted to hit one more twenty yard grounder." – Jim Bishop

This is a second chance shot, which Bruce uses quite often. In fact, as often as possible. If at any time the ball does not go in the right direction or if it is left sitting on or just adjacent to the green, then a Mulligan is the answer. Just in case you did not know golf can be a game of highs and lows. In most cases for the beginner or weekend hacker, the ball does not always do what it is supposed to do. Funny about that.

THE PREFERRED LIE

This has nothing to do with lying. This is when a ball lands in an area that is playable only with great difficulty that Bruce takes advantage of his new rule. That is to move the ball to a more advantageous position.

If the ball is laying in a hollow or divot then it is carefully picked up and paced on the highest tussock of grass, which would act as nature's own tee. From there a swing is taken and watch out.

BUNKER SHOT

If at first you don't succeed try and try again. Don't forget you have your spade too, you may need it. You are not supposed to touch the sand when lining up your ball while in the bunker, but Bruce uses the dead ground to hastily dig around and make sure that his ball is clear for that swing of his. He has even been known to raise the ball up slightly, on a little mound that he has a habit of building. He has always been keen on sandcastles ever since he was a little kid on Bondi Beach.

However, when no one is looking you can, either pick up your ball and then throw it, or if you can't get away with that then your right golf shoe with Bruce's handy Florsheim wedge, stuck to the toe comes into its own.

8

GOLF TERMINOLOGY

"Putts get real difficult the day they hand out the money." – Lee Trevino

Although they speak a sort of English our American cousins have different terminology

As with most sports or pastimes like sailing, football, cricket or baseball, golf has its own language. To the non-player, this language is puzzling and sometimes one of amusement. An attempt to explain what these golf terms mean are shown below in this list:

Ace - When a player hits the ball directly from the tee into the hole with one stroke. Also called a 'hole in one.' Just dreams for most players, but something we all strive for.

Approach Shot - A shot intended to land the ball on the green. This is where a lot of hope and prayer comes into it.

Apron – On the edge of the green. If you are lucky, your ball will land here and not into the rough.

Away – Crazy, this is where some kind of etiquette comes into play. The player whose ball is furthest from the flag gets to putt first.

Back Nine – Okay so you're tired. This is the second nine holes in the course. Your back is hurting and the clubhouse bar is beckoning.

Backswing – Just before you hit the ball, keep it slow.

Ball-marker – Just so you can remember where your ball was on the green. Try to avoid the temptation to move it forward.

Ball-washer – A handy gizmo to wash all that mud off your ball. Bruce likes to play with that.

Best Ball – Bruce has never had one of these.

The Birdie - One under par. Bruce has always been keen on birds and often consults with his bird book on what bird he sees on the golf course. However, the Birdie has continued to elude him but he is always hopeful.

The Albatross - Three under par. Buckley's. No chance, at all!

Backspin - No hope here. Bruce has never tried it, as he has enough trouble hitting the ball properly in the first place and finding the elusive sweet-spot on the clubface. This shot is supposed to bring the ball up short and sometimes roll back

GOLF – THE TRUE STORY

when it lands. Bruce has never ever come close to mastering this one.

Bombs - He once had a car that was a bit of a bomb, but has no idea what a golf shot called a bomb does. He will look it up on the Internet and let you know.

Bogey – A very familiar situation for Bruce, where he is one shot over par for a hole.

Break – This is another familiar problem with Bruce and is where his ball doesn't roll straight into the cup. He then blames it on a leaf, a twig, the greenkeeper and bumpy bits on the green.

Bump and Run – See 'Grasscutter', designed to roll the ball closer to the flag.

Bunker – Designed by sadists. Also called a sand trap or a !@#$%^&*!

Caddy – a sometimes irritating person who carries your bag.

Carry – This is how far the ball wings its way down the fairway (or bounces).

Casual Water – Puddles.

Chip – Sometimes a snack that comes in a bag. However, in golf it is a shot designed to lob the ball onto the green and roll it into the cup. Laughable.

Chunk – Where your clubface decides to become a shovel and you dig a bit of grass and soil, "the chunk," – which goes further than your ball.

Club – Where they serve the beers. Or the crazily designed implement you are supposed to hit a golf ball with.

Clubhead – The bumpy bit on the end of your club which you use to hit a ball.

Clubface – The flat bit on the bumpy bit.

Course Rating – The number of shots the sadists reckon you should hit per hole.

Dimples – The little round dents in the golf ball. The other marks are from chewing, hitting and other misadventures. They are supposed to make your ball carry further. What a joke!

Divot – See 'Chunk', remember to carry a bucket of sand to hide your sins.

Dogleg – Part of the hazards of a golf course where the fairway is crooked.

Double Bogey – Two shots over par. Very familiar number.

Double Eagle – A lot of shots under par for the hole. Wasting time writing about this one!

Downswing – Alright, you have brought your Club back and when you let fly, that is a Downswing. Keep your head down also.

Draw – Often done by amateurs, although the Pro's work that into the game and show off. They can make their ball go anywhere.

Drop - Bruce reckons he has dropped more than a club and ball, in fact, he has almost dropped the whole lot of his kit in the lake at 'The Lakes' golf course near Sydney. Bruce sometimes calls this a lob or an air shot. The ball goes up and then plummets to the ground, usually digging itself deeply into the turf.

Eagle - Two under par. For Bruce, the chance of getting an Eagle is about the same as getting a date with Jennifer Lopez, or becoming Prime Minister.

Even – Like a par. Ha Ha!

Fade – The better golfers can do this and curve their ball around a dogleg fairway. Bruce can do this but not when he wants to.

Fairway – The long bit of grass area between when you tee off and stagger to the next flag.

Flagstick – Sometimes gets in the way of a lucky putt. It looks good on a windy day.

Flop Shot - "Hell, said Bruce, I flop a lot, but I am sure that they don't mean this when they say he hit a flop shot." That's right Bruce, this shot is one that is far out of the expertise you have shown on the golf links.

Fore – Didn't know it was spelt like this. This is shouted when you hit the ball and you see that it may be heading in the direction of people. Also 'Look out', 'duck' or 'watch it' can do if you can't remember 'fore'.

GOLF – THE TRUE STORY

Foursomes – Four guys playing together, telling fibs about their score.

Front Nine – This comes before the back nine. But if you're playing at 'Coonabarabran Golf Course' (NSW country town), it is called the "Only Nine".

Gimme – Where two players are having a bad day and both of them have another shot which is not counted.

Golf Club – The badly designed thing that you are supposed to hit your golf ball with. You can carry 14 of them, long ones and short ones, but in Bruce's case they don't make a lot of difference.

Grasscutter – this is when you mishit the ball and instead of rising, it skims the grass down the fairway.

Green – The colour of grass, silly! Also, the thing you aim for with a flagpole stuck in it.

Handicap – Bruce has a few of these. After this, it gets a bit complicated.

Hole – This is where you want to get the ball into with as few shots as possible. But, remember to take the flagpole out first. It helps.

Hole in One - As Humphrey Bogart said in the movie, "The Maltese Falcon", it's what dreams are made of. Humph was supposed to be talking about the value of the Maltese Falcon, but Bruce thinks he may have been referring to his other love, that of the game of golf and the possibility of achieving a hole in one.

Iron – Clubs that are made entirely of metal stuff. They are usually numbered from 1 to 9.

Kangaroo Hop – Called this in Australia. You mishit the ball and it bounces down the fairway while you hope it keeps on going.

Knock-down – If it's windy, try and keep your shot low to the ground, otherwise, you have an excuse for it going crooked.

Lie – You would think this is about fibbing and boy is there a lot of that going on around a golf course. However, it is supposed to mean that is where your ball is lying. This is when you need to work out how to play the next shot.

Line – Where the ball is supposed to go. Remember to not walk in front of your mate who is putting on his line, that could be a bit of gamesmanship, hey!

Links – A golf course with a chain of fairways.

Loft – Most golf clubs have their face at an angle, designed to give your ball a lift.

Lost Ball – Some players don't own up to this and drop a spare. The scenario is thus. You have hooked the ball and it is somewhere in the rough. Despite your best intentions, you cannot find the little bugger, even though it is coloured bright pink. Luckily you have a few more of the same balls in your pocket and Bruce usually drops one of these, in this situation, right on the edge of the fairway and exclaims, "Well, blow me down, here it is hiding right in front of me."

Now, Bruce feels pretty guilty about this, but after all, he is playing against himself and seeking no handicap.

Mulligan - A do-over, or replay of the shot, without counting the shot as a stroke and without assessing any penalties that might apply. It is not allowed by the rules and not practised in official tournaments, but is common in casual rounds in some countries, especially the United States.

Natural Hazzard - Our hero Bruce makes much of this golfing aid. The groundsman leaves his curled up hose near the green, the trench dug possibly dug by some Army Corp, the puddle of water, the temporary metre high fence stuck into the ground by some helpful greenkeeper and much more, all are there to make a golfer's lot a tough one.

Bruce, however, ever the optimist, uses these hazards to get closer to the flag. The fumble as he drops the ball, which somehow carries a good five metres is something that he has perfected.

Nineteenth Hole - The clubhouse bar. Players typically gather in the 19th Hole after their round to tally scores, settle bets and enjoy some beverages. (And sometimes lie a little).

Out-of-bounds – The ball is hit and goes wild. This could end up with a penalty stroke ordered against you.

Par – This is where the sadists who designed the course, have deemed a good player obtains a standard score.

Pin – That's another name for the flagpole stuck in the middle of the green.

Pitch – A cricket pitch, or in golf a shot that is required to go only a short distance towards the hole.

Pitch Mark – These little blighters are where a golf ball drops and makes a neat crater in the ground. Excellent excuse if you manage to putt and hit one.

Play Through – You are playing behind a foursome that is slow. Agonisingly slow. If you stand there with your hands on your hips, frown and grumble enough they may get the hint and invite you to go ahead of them and play, thus leaving them behind for the next lot of players to contend with.

Pro – No silly quip here. You know what a Pro is. In fact, there is a whole section devoted to them in this book.

Punch Shot – This is where you are in amongst trees and you try and hit your ball low to avoid branches. Any other time you hit low and this time when you want to, the ball goes high and hits a tree and bounces back. A little bit of cursing then takes place, @#$$%^&*!

Putt – You're on the green so use your putter, mate!

Putting Green – This is where you practice your putting. Possibly the most important place in golf.

GOLF – THE TRUE STORY

Putter – A golf club with a vertical face, designed again by engineers with sadistic tendencies, for putting and their fellow man.

Rough – Yes, it can be rough if you venture off the fairway.

Sand Wedge – A club used to get under the ball and lift it towards the cup. Never works much.

Scramble – Running around in circles trying to finish the game so you can get to the clubhouse for a cold one.

Scratch Golfer – This is where you sometimes meet a player, who hits off with a handicap of nil. They may be aliens.

Shamble – I don't know. Could be when the four of you chose the best shot for a score.

Shank – this is when the ball hits the hosel (where the club is attached to the handle) of the club, nearly missing the clubface entirely. This is when you start swearing a bit

Short Game Shots – Like putting if you get good at this, then you are on your way to being a good golfer.

Slice – This is when your ball goes off on a mind of its own and ends up to the right of you, usually in the next fairway.

Tap-in – This is when your ball is really close to the edge of the cup. Your mates may allow you to tap the ball in.

Tee – This is what you usually balance your ball on when you are teeing off.

Topped – Many golfers have experienced this shot. It is when you lift your head and you hit the top of the ball, causing it to bounce away down the fairway. The trick is, to make it look like you played it that way or you don't care that it was a duffer of a shot anyway.

Unplayable – If you own up to this and have another shot they still want to penalise you one stroke. Spoilsports.

Up and Down – Chip onto the green and then one putt, you beauty!

Wedge - A type of golf club designed to lift your ball and lob it closer to the flag. The inventor was most probably smoking grass and don't mean the stuff you find on the fairway.

Whiff – Declared a 'Practice Swing' by many this is where you try and hit the ball and miss. The trick is to look nonchalant and just carry on as if nothing has happened.
Wood – This is the big club usually made of wood. They don't hit too straight either.

9

PEOPLE WHO PLAY GOLF

Golf tips are like Aspirin: One may do you good, but if you swallow the whole bottle you'll be lucky to survive." Harvey Penick

In a previous chapter, we briefly looked at the history of golf and now address the types of people who play the game. In fact, unlike the game of a few generations ago, it is now a very democratic game and all manner of people play it. There is no typical type that's for sure. Since the early days of golf, the game has gradually changed, while the people who play it have also changed.

In the early days, it was the wealthy who played golf, however, today anybody who can beg borrow or steal a set of golf clubs can play. We are lucky in Australia where there are a lot of public golf courses which makes the game available to everyone for a very modest sum.

It has often been of interest to Bruce to look at other stalwarts who front up to the golf course when he is there. They come in all shapes and sizes. In fact, all types of the human species most probably. Coming from a sales background, Bruce enjoys looking at people and he fancies that he can identify what their profession is or the type of person they are. Most salesmen are amateur psychologists anyhow. Basically,, he thinks that the following types are typical. Do you think you can recognise anyone you know? So, here we go...

THE BEGINNER

> *"I know I am getting better at golf because I am hitting fewer players."* – Gerald R. Ford, the 38th President of the USA

You can always tell when a beginner is about to play. They have been taking golf lessons from Chuck at the Pro Shop. They hunker down, tuck in their bottom after waggling it a few times. Keep their head down, bring their club back slowly and then red-faced and sweating they launch into action. All this is taken in slow motion and absolutely painful to watch. Phut goes the ball and kangaroo hops away down the straight sixty metres before coming to rest in the long grass of the rough behind a tree. Beginners still swear, unlike the stoic professional.

This fellow is also, not always sure which club to use. Many times he chants quietly, 'eenie, meenie, miney, moe' and grabs any stick that looks like it will do the job.

Leaning down to place the golf ball adroitly on its tee. No problem for a talented amateur but to the Beginner, well the tee does not go into the ground straight. The ball is placed carefully. Then he or she goes to hit it and halfway through the swing the ball over-balances and drops off the tee. A little rage is allowed here though, as the ball placing ceremony is

GOLF – THE TRUE STORY

repeated a couple of times. Anyone looking on is either pretending to look elsewhere or is impatient, as they can see their golf day slipping way. Nobody wants to get stuck behind this player.

Harvey stood there and wondered what club would produce success.

The hook or the slice is a familiar shot for this player too. If only it could be done the same every time they hit, then they could go around any dog leg hole on the course. However, no luck. When this player goes to hit a slice on purpose, the ball goes straight and you guessed it, ends up deep in the bush on the side of the fairway.

Getting out of a bunker is also a big problem for this golfer. Some of these sandy hollows are evil and have a 'lip' overhanging the sand and tends to be always in between the ball and the flag. A few 'practice swings', red faces, a lot of swearing and a bit of praying leads to the golfer picking up his ball and throwing it.

Lost balls, bent clubs, hazards and bunkers all test the mettle of any beginner. Is it any wonder that so many sets of golf clubs lie gathering dust in thousands of garages throughout the Western World. The golf club manufacturers know this and rub their hands in glee as they count their profits.

THE HACKER

"If you're caught on a golf course during a storm and are afraid of lightning, hold up a 1-iron. Not even God can hit a 1-iron." – Lee Trevino

This type of player is the *occasional* golfer. Our hero Bruce is in this category; his opportunity to play golf coming up say only 6 times a year. It's not enough for him to get any better at the game. Mind you, he lives in hope.

The earnest desire by this occasional golfer to be good at the game, is negated by the very few times that he plays.

The old saying, "Practice Makes Perfect", does not apply here. Usually, this golfer has other more pressing matters to attend to, rather than spend the whole of Saturday at the golf course. He has the grandchildren to see, a list of odd jobs to do around the house supervised by the memsahib who keeps a very short rein on him. Although, far more important priorities like seeing his mates down at the pub for a game of darts or a few coldies takes precedence.

Bruce was not going to give in. He was still out there.

Not only does he not play often, but he is a seasonal golfer. Summer is far too hot for this fellow. What with the flies and the threat of a severe case of sunburn.

Winter is far too cold and usually raining or windy. Thus Bruce and his ilk tend to play a round or two during spring or autumn. These seasons here in Australia are far too short and so the golf clubs remain sitting in the garage, waiting for a chance to get out and play.

However, as with many golfers, the Hacker is reluctant to give in when the weather is bad. Rain, wind and hail make no difference, the Hacker hangs in there. Bruce has been known to be a little slow in playing his 18 holes. Lost balls, multiple putts and a lot of swearing ends up seeing him still playing as the sun is setting.

Never mind, Bruce stays out there determined to get his monies worth.

Or as one anonymous funnyman said, "If you do find that you do not mind playing golf in the rain, the snow, even during a hurricane, here's a valuable tip: Your life is in trouble."

THE TALENTED AMATEUR

"You don't know what pressure is until you play for five bucks with only two in your pocket." – Lee Trevino, again

Bruce particularly envies this type of golfer. They have been blessed with a natural swing, perfect eye-hand coordination and playoff 3 or 4. This is usually genetic, as their family are known as talented sportsmen. Excelling at all things involving a ball. Cricket, tennis, or softball, all come easy to the talented amateur. The closest thing that Bruce got with ball games was when he rolled Jaffa's (an orange coated chocolate ball candy) down the aisle on a Saturday afternoon at the local flicks, where all the children watched that week's movie serials.

He realises that is why he has no natural aptitude for the game, but still perseveres with the hope that one day he will have a breakthrough and play like his hero Garry Player.

It always came easy to Owen, but adding up his scorecard was kind of difficult.

On the other hand one of Bruce's mates, Owen has always been a natural sport. A champion tennis player, lawn bowl exponent, cricketer and of course a mean golfer with a low handicap. Wearing shorts to show off his well-muscled legs, which need a liberal dose of 'Aerogard' (an Australian insect repellent), in summer coz the flies and mozzies love Owen's legs.

Owen wore a two-toned pair of golf shoes; a conservative polo shirt, showing off his splendid torso; and a Terry Towelling bucket hat, to soak up any stray drops of perspiration on his follicly-challenged head. The 'Talented Amateur' looked every inch a champion.

Just on sundown, when all sensible players are at the 19th hole downing a few cold ones, Owen is still out there getting his monies worth. Coincidentally, that is 'Zero Hour' where squadrons of giant mosquitoes swarm and all head for Owen's bulging calves.

The first you know about the problem our 'Talented Amateur" is experiencing, is the sound of groaning and slapping. Gone is the desire to play on those last few holes. Gone is the longing to attain just one more par. Gone is Owen's thirst for glory.

Bruce is suddenly left *all* alone with the night clouds darkening the sky, and all that can be heard is the clanking of his mates' clubs in their bags, as they race headlong toward the safety of the clubhouse, followed by swarms of ravenous mozzies of course.

Lucky old Bruce follows sedately behind smirking to himself and thinking that the 'Big O' is short of vitamin B or something. As he read somewhere, that is why mosquitoes are drawn to one person as against another.

Bruce may not be a good golfer but he is safe from the mosquito's dive-bombing nearby.

THE PROFESSIONAL

"The reason a pro tells you to keep your head down is so you can't see him laughing." – Phyllis Diller

Like the talented amateur, this player is blessed with the right genes. And I don't mean 'Levis'. Somewhere in Heaven, God is sitting on his throne laughing at a few of his creations (the Hacker) and smiles with satisfaction and nods his head knowingly, when he watches the professionals play golf.

Phil stood there in all his glory with his loyal caddie looking on.

When Bruce had the misfortune to play a game of golf with the champion amateur, Phil Billings, some years ago, he managed to lose his ball a few times, hit 12 on the first hole and generally made an ass of himself. Phil kindly looked down from his height (he was tall as well as handsome) and said, "Never mind Bruce, if you aim at the target often enough, you will eventually hit it."

A word of warning dear reader. Do not play golf with someone who is a 'scratch golfer'. For anyone who wants to know what this supreme-being is, well he or she is someone who has around a zero handicap. This means that the player will usually shoot right around par on any given course. That is unless you have a low handicap also.

It can be disheartening when they tee off with the usual smooth swing, as the ball streaks away down the middle of the fairway. Or they putt with deadly accuracy and so on. Mind you in addition to God's gift of the right genes, they play regularly and work hard at their game.

You can't expect to be a champion if you only play once every three months. Now can you?

How many of you watch golf on TV and are inspired to do better. The Pro's make it look easy don't they. Well it isn't. And remember the immortal words ....

"Golf is a cow of a game." – Anonymous player

Editor's Note: Phil Billings has won the 'Lake Macquarie Amateur' the most times, winning on seven occasions (1959, 1960, 1961, 1964, 1965, 1966, and 1974), and was the medallist in the 1961 'Australian Amateur'. Billings also competed in professional events. He won the 1961 'Lakes Open' and was a runner-up in the 1971 'New South Wales Open'. Bruce wants to be like Phil.

GOLF – THE TRUE STORY

THE ARTIST

"Some golfers, we are told, enjoy the landscape; but properly, the landscape shrivels and compresses into the grim, surrealistically vivid patch of grass directly under the golfer's eyes as he morosely walks toward where he thinks his ball might be." – John Updike

This player whether a he or she tends to be flamboyant and creative. Silk scarf at the neck, gaily coloured smock, paint-spattered trousers, the sandals and with, of course, the jaunty French beret. This golfer looks for different things in the game of golf, unlike the other golfing types. This player is a nature lover.

Claude could see the scene before him was worthy of one of his masterpieces.

They are fervently interested in the wildlife on the course and the game takes second place. For example a sighting of a mob of Apostle Birds or a Blue Wren sends them into a frenzy. They may even drop their clubs and reach for a camera or a sketch pad to record the moment. Fervently vowing, that when they get home they will look up their bird book for the details of their sighting.

All these amateur Ecologists doings result in their game suffering, as their concentration is shot. They can't get back into the game after sighting a rabbit, a fox, a wallaby or a possum. Their heart pounds and they have a vision as to how they would paint a picture, compose a poem or a song to commemorate the occasion.

Meanwhile, their fellow golfers give sideways glances of dismay, as the artist waffles on about the benefits of the coloured plumage of a King parrot or the russet tones of a stray dog, which he insists is a European red fox.

The shape of the clouds. Gorgeous. The autumn leaves fluttering down on a gentle breeze. Dazzling. A gaudy sunset sends our creative player into raptures.

All of this behaviour fills his fellow players with despair, as the game becomes slower and slower until our hero is off with his cell phone taking photos of the flora and fauna. They dream of being another David Attenborough and having their article and photos published in the 'National Geographic' magazine.

By now you will have guessed that the creative golfer, is not in the same league as the Military Man or the Engineer type. The artist gene in this gofer tends to see that their game is more important to them as an artistic creation, rather than a careful attempt to reduce one's handicap. No attempt to improve how one plays just the sheer joy of being out in the open air with Mother Nature.

One of the most fun things to do for this player is to rake the bunker. In his mind's eye, he can see how the Japanese treat their Zen garden beds of gravel and sand. He would spend a considerable amount of time, if permitted, in doing this with the bunkers on the course.

Green is their favourite colour. (Editor's Note: I told you they were different.)

THE DANDY

> *"If golfers know they look good, they will play better. I think that is valid for men and women."* – Letitia Baldrige

This is the guy or gal who dress for the occasion. They have the most up to date golf fashion. Their clothes are designer-made and their shoes are two-toned with the obligatory double tassels.

Their kit and caboodle is new, clean and sparkling. This fellow is the one with all the best gear. Fancy two tone shoes with super-size cleats that not only give him a good grip on things but he helps the greenkeeper in aerating the soil.

Dressed in immaculate lolly pink strides and a sparkling white polo shirt. Smart golf shoes that match his state of the art golf bag. Anyone within the vicinity will know that it would be a mortal sin to hit a ball anywhere near this splendid being.

A nifty new cap from America, also a bright colour, and guaranteed to repel any mad magpie who wants to dive bomb him at nesting time.

Only the best kid glove on Kurt's left hand which aids his grip on the stick and ensures that his hands have no wear and blisters.

Kurt was a Dandy and was sure that dressing well would make him a better player

Some years ago Bruce was invited to have a game with a visiting Swiss Banker at 'Royal Turramurra Club' (Sydney). They arranged to meet at the golf course and Bruce met up with Kurt on the first tee. Poor Bruce was ashamed to look at his gear, compared to the red and white bag with shiny and sparkling clubs with covers and tassels all colour coordinated. Kurt was beautifully dressed for the occasion too. Bruce looked at his second-hand kit. A tatty mustard plastic bag, mismatched clubs and no covers for his clubs. His clothes consisted of jeans with sneakers and a tee-shirt emblazoned with the logo of the local Dairy Milk Company, 'Creamy Udders'.

Bruce invited Kurt to start off. The tall and handsome Swiss gave a few practice swings and he was a picture of elegance and competence. Then Kurt got serious and gave a swipe and the ball soared to the right and hit a fellow in the ankle on the next fairway.

Bruce looked heavenward and said a silent prayer along the lines of, "I now know there is a God."

This is a classic case where clothes definitely do not make the man, or the player for that matter. Most probably though the Dandy likes all the designer gear or else their partner buys their clothes for them.

Thankfully there are never too many Dandies on the golf courses here in Australia although if you travel to the good old USA you will see hordes of them. Checked pants, plus fours, crazy caps and golf bags gleaming with chrome.

Perhaps this famous golfer has the last say here.

"Nobody asked how you looked, just what you shot." Sam Snead.

STEVE MCGREGOR

THE COUNTRY BOY

"The most important shot in golf is the next one." – Ben Hogan

This golfer arrives at the course with his borrowed clubs. He has to scrounge some golf balls and is quick to grab any stray plastic tee laying in the grass. His pants are moleskins, a bush shirt and he spurns golf shoes, vowing to never wear anything except his elastic sided boots all shaded by his wide-brimmed hat.

GOLF – THE TRUE STORY

Ralph is ready for anything and makes sure he knows where the 19th hole is.

The Country Boy is used to many conditions that would make a city born golfer blanch. He has learned to ignore drought, flies and the kangaroos that seek out the green grass of the golf course. Mind you the wild pigs make a hell of a mess on the putting greens. Bruce often thinks that it would be a good idea to include a .303 rifle in his golf bag for those sightings of any feral pigs that can sometimes be found rooting around near the green on the eleventh hole.

After all, in many places in the bush, it is pretty dry so carrying an umbrella is a waste of space. The loops could easily be modified to accommodate a rifle. Ammo could be kept in one of the buggy's pockets.

Bruce has an affinity for this golfer, as he too lived for a time in the outback near Enngonia on 'Boolaroo' sheep station where he trained as a Jackeroo.

Most country towns have their own golf course, though sometimes just 9 holes. The town of Dunedoo, in NSW's west had a problem recently. A disgruntled player took a bulldozer to the golf course and wiped out many of the green and ruined a few fairways. At the last 'Stop Press' we believe that the local constable is pursuing a masked golfer driving a tractor. The only problem here is that the constable is a trifle overweight and his bicycle is a tad slower than the tractor, so no arrest has been forthcoming to date.

The Dunedoo golfers have now had to relocate their golf game to the neighbouring town like Coonabarabran, until their Dunedoo golf course is repaired. Strange things happen to the Country Boy.

He would also have to change a few things if he were to come down to the 'Big Smoke" and play on a Sydney golf course. For a start, no rifle in his bag and he must leave his handy pocketknife at home.

The police don't want any crazy Country Boy taking after the greenkeeper, who neglected to clear a few natural hazards, with a knife now do we?

THE OLD GEEZER

> *"The only sure rule in golf is he who has the fastest golf cart never has to play the bad lie."* – Mickey Mantle, baseball champ

On any given day you will see the golf courses crammed with old geezers. For you see, the younger generation, in most cases, do not have the time to play golf.

They are sitting at home playing golf on their computers or iPads. This is much easier you see, less expensive too. Or they are being taxi drivers to their children on sports days, which regretfully fall on a Saturday, so that makes the weekend golf game, a tough call for young married folks.

The Old Geezer usually dresses in plus fours with a nifty golf cap, and he drives an electric buggy. He makes sure that he has an adequate water supply, with some paracetamol tablets: for those aches-and-pains.

He plays every week on the same golf links, with the same foursome, and his game has not varied one iota over the last 50 years.

The old boy is a golfer who has played for decades and is religiously trying to play to his handicap. His handicap nowadays though is arthritis, piles and a new knee which still gives him moments of discomfort.

Alf's wife is pleased he leaves for golf and plays all day and comes home tuckered out to sleep in front of the TV. After 60 years of marriage, she welcomes the peace and quiet.

Alfred also enjoys the fellowship after the game and sits in a corner sipping on his 'Carlton Draught' beer while exchanging insults and tall tales with his mates.

Alfred has played for years but sometimes forgets where the next hole is.

One of his very great pleasures in life is to flirt with young Marie, the barmaid, who stoically puts up with the weak puns, jokes that never get to the punchline and small tips that would not help her with the payment of her mortgage.

The Old Geezer has a saying which he often says to anyone who stops to chat. "Old Golfers never die, they just fade away."

Did you hear the one about the Old Geezer?

"How was your golf game dear?" asks Alfred's wife.

"I was hitting pretty well, but my eyesight's so bad I couldn't see where the ball went."

"You're 75 years old now, Alfred, why don't you take my brother Scott along?" suggests his wife.

"But he's 85 and doesn't even play golf anymore," protests Alfred.

"But he's got perfect eyesight. He could watch your ball," his wife points out.

The next day Alfred tees off with Scott looking on. Alfred swings and the ball disappears into the rough of the fairway.

"Do you see it?" asks Alfred.

"Yup," Scott answers.

"Well, where is it?" Yells Alfred, peering off into the distance.

"I forget."

THE MILITARY MAN

> *"What other people may find in poetry or art museums, I find in the flight of a good drive."* – Arnold Palmer

The complete antithesis to the Artist type. Now, Bruce has seen these chaps, marching around the golf course as if keeping in time to a distant drum. Military bearing, guardsman moustache, obligatory Diggers hat and clothes similar to the Australian military's SD's (Service Dress), light khaki coloured pants shirt with the deep pockets.

The Major treated the ball as if it was a live hand grenade

Bruce always watches closely to see what the Military Man has in those bulging pockets. He would not be at all surprised to see K rations, a canteen of water, ammunition cleaning kit and so on appear as well as all the bits and bobs relating to golf.

Bruce has also observed, that they carry their golf club as if it is a Lee Enfield rifle and treat the golf ball as if it was a live hand grenade.

Sometimes it is not a lot of fun being part of a foursome with the ex-Army officer types. They still think they are on parade and bark at you, if you have the temerity to talk or show any humour.

Heaven help you if you sneeze or miss-hit a ball into the rough when he is about to tee off. Bruce has the answer though with this type of player. He virtually hides while the Major is about to hit a ball. He stands behind one of the other players with his back to the action. That keeps him out of harm's way.

Bruce makes sure that he never meets the Major's piercing gaze. He will do anything not to incur his displeasure, in fact, he is scared of the Major.

This fellow prepares for his golf game as if it is a military exercise. Logistics are important to the military man. No doubt there is a checklist somewhere, when he is getting ready for a game. Clothes, rations, equipment, buggy (oiled wheels, check), ammo and so on.

Bruce suspects that the Major's wife, just like the Old Geezer's, is damn glad to see her husband march off to the golf course each week. Peace reigns in the house while she sits back in the kitchen with her slippers on, drinking Lanchoo tea, sucking on an arrowroot biscuit and smoking a Craven A cigarette.

The Major has gone off to golf to make others miserable.

THE CLOWN

"I once played a course that was so tough, I lost two balls in the ball washer!" – Anonymous. *(Okay, so it was a lame old joke but that is the level that this type of player stoops to.)*

Now, The Clown player can be a real curse on the golf course. When you are concentrating on your game, this fellow chooses that time to tell a joke. Then he has the nerve to laugh uproariously at the punch line.

Frankie thought it was a great joke and dissolved into peals of laughter.

Everything is funny to the joker. Lame jokes, smart remarks, criticisms of various media identities, the latest gossip about a politician and practical jokes all are grist to the mill for Frankie.

You see he was complimented by his adoring grandma when Frankie was five years of age after telling her the latest joke from school. The appreciation of his wit was the catalyst for his life as a joker, wag, clown and amateur comedian.

The problem is that although he was funny at the age of five, his sense of humour has not changed since then. Alas,

GOLF – THE TRUE STORY

so many of his audience would have cause to curse grandma ever since.

Everything is fun to Frank. Golf is not meant to be serious. A ball ending up in the lagoon. Peals of laughter. A miss-hit and a ball kangaroo hopping down the fairway, gales of laughter and slapping everyone on the back. The incessant chatter and joking around never ceases and makes it very difficult for the other members of the foursome to concentrate.

No one has the heart to tell Frankie, that he is a very naughty boy and so the litany of woe goes on.

Now, for the practical jokes. Frank thought it would be funny to help out one of his short-sighted fellow players and bent down to clear some grass away from his ball, while quickly swapping balls.

When his fellow player teed up and hit the ball of chalk you can imagine the scene. A cloud of white powder, pieces of ball scattered around and a look of shock on all the players, while Frank bent over, in a guffaw of laughter.

Another time Frank had bored a hole in a golf ball and inserted a screw eye and then tied a piece of nylon fishing line to it.

Again he swapped balls with a fellow player and when the man came to swing, he had hold of the fishing line and whipped the ball away before the club hit the ball.

Again gales of laughter and dark looks from all present.

Plastic snakes, fake spiders and even fake turds have all been deposited for Frank's unfortunate fellow golfers. One of his favourite pranks was to shine a laser light on the ball and watch the mystified expression on his fellow golfer's face.

Frank did have a dream and that was to get a fart balloon and use that, so he was looking forward to next week's game. He could just imagine what would happen when his mate was about to hit off and he let go of the fart. When everybody stopped to listen for another one, Frank thought that the real joke was to blame it on his mate. He thought that would be funny.

Mind you eventually their good humour and excuses for his behaviour will be eventually overcome and Frank will either be given a stern talking to or even given his marching orders.

They may even forget to invite him.

Frankie may not be amused.

THE PLAYER WITH A SHORT FUSE

> *"Golf! You hit down to make the ball go up. You swing left and the damn ball goes right. The lowest score wins. And, on top of that, the winner buys the drinks!"* – Anonymous, but definitely an angry player.

We have all played at some time with a fellow like this. Woe betide you if you say anything remotely different to this man's strict code or politics. During the remainder of the 18 holes, conversation dries up to a minimum and the game degenerates into a trial of minds with tension on all. Bruce eventually becoming so anxious that he plays even worse than usual. This is a vicious circle, as the worse Bruce plays the grumpier this fellow gets, until Bruce longs for the cool comforts of the clubhouse.

The solution to this situation is for Bruce to claim that he has done his back in and retire gracefully to the clubhouse for a cool beer until the remaining three finish their trial of tears. By this time and after a few beers, Bruce is very relaxed and after telling a few jokes that don't go over too well, wends his way off home.

You can see that this angry golfer should be avoided at all costs. They tend to say and do things that may offend you. Even worse, you may end up with a thrown golf ball decorating your ear or even worse, a 3-iron wrapped around your scrawny neck.

How many times have you been walking around hunting for your ball in the rough when you have come across a bent or broken club. Guess who left it there? Well, of course, it is this angry fellow who takes his dose of rage out on his golf club.

It is assumed that at some time in your playing life, you have felt like jumping up and down on your golf kit. Now, own up guys and gals. Because, well, golf can be a frustrating game.

Just imagine things are going swimmingly and you're heading towards one of those few holes where you are on track for that elusive par. And with great confidence, you select your 8-iron to lob a ball close to the flag for an easy putt, when disaster happens…

William stood there grinding his teeth as his blood pressure rose alarmingly

For some reason, perhaps the mischievous God of golf has decided to play one of the game's tricks on you. Your ball, instead of sailing gracefully heavenward and then stuttering to a halt near the flag, goes off at a crazy angle and instead of getting that par, you now know that you will be lucky to finish this hole with a few shots over par.

Not to worry, it simply can't happen again. Well, don't you believe it?

Golf balls just have a mind of their own, don't they? When you least expect it, the ball whizzes off on its own trajectory with no rhyme or reason. That is when the player gets a bit antsy.

Bruce has felt like this every so often but his continued state of penury ensures that he cares for his clubs as he doesn't want to go to the expense of buying more. Breaking clubs or even bending these badly designed tools is a "no-no".

Usually, we don't mind the sight of a player jumping up and down, smashing a club, bending a club around a tree and yelling in rage. However, it is the sobbing and crying that gets to you in these cases.

THE LADIES

> *"Golf is a compromise between what your ego wants you to do, what experience tells you to do, and what your nerves let you do."* – Bruce Crampton

The old girls are usually a little slow to get around the course. For some reason, they wish to avoid Ladies Day and play a round on a Saturday. Drives of 80 metres are the maximum and a major number of balls end up in the rough.

Nothing gets these players down, however, and they religiously hunt for every ball that ends up in the rough. While this is going on the players cued up behind, shift from one foot to another while murmuring vile oaths under their breaths.

The shrieks of laughter and never-ending drone of conversation is heard echoing around the golf course also leading to bouts of high blood pressure, hair loss and aggravated piles by the older players. Many a golf course has a memorial to some old geezer who had an attack of high blood pressure leading to a fatal heart attack, because of the delays.

Betty and Dotty played every weekend and enjoyed their walk and talk.

When approached by the Club manager to suggest that the ladies change their habits and explained the effect they had on the old members.

Betty laughed and said, "Goodness they are always so impatient. Do you think I should go and talk to them?"

They have hit on a clever game plan to achieve a better score. If they hit into the rough, for example, they quickly place their ball on a tee and hit the ball. If this is done quickly enough, the other two in their foursome do not notice. By doing this stratagem, they are able to hit that pesky ball quite a way and avoid digging in with their clubhead resulting in a fizzer or a grass cutter.

It is a little easier for the Ladies too. They tee off from the Ladies Tees. For anyone who asks why are they called 'Ladies Tees'? Well, the average male golfer hits the ball farther than the average female golfer, which means that women are more likely to choose a set of tees that is more forward (or shorter in terms of distance from tee to green).

And what happens if you don't hit it past the ladies tees? Regardless, the premise of the rule is that if a male player's drive does not make it past the forward or more commonly known as the ladies tees, that male player must play the rest of the hole with his "club" hanging out of his pants.

THE SWEET YOUNG THING

> *"Give me golf clubs, fresh air and a beautiful partner, and you can keep the clubs and the fresh air."* – Jack Benny

These players are not that common. See Chapter 14, 'Distractions in Golf' section in this book.

Mind you when you least expect it, they are seen on the golf course. Decorative, supple and sensuous creatures dressed scantily in tight clothes. (Editor's note: had to pause here in the narrative a bit).

These sweet young things sometimes inhabit the golf links but do not stay long. Invariably some old geezer will stroll over to see if he can give them some tips or a gifted amateur will offer to fill up their sand bucket. In no time a crowd gathers of silent staring men, in all shapes and sizes, all eager to help.

Deidre blushed as she stood there aware of all the old boys looking on.

The young ladies will suffer all this attention in silence, while they stand there and do some warm-up exercises. While this is all going on, their silent audience of sweaty golfers are lined up neglecting their own games.

They just happen to be there you see and as to where they have come from nobody knows, but they seem to be attracted to the sweet young things as bees to honey.

After their warm-up stretches and so on the girls, amid some self-conscious giggles, at all the attention, wander over to tee off.

After this is done there is a collective sigh from the audience, as if a hundred of them have been holding their breath. Now, that could not be.

Okay, now, let's get serious for a moment. There are quite a lot of professional female golfers and they in many cases look gorgeous. This then shows that despite their film star looks; they play well, in fact, extremely well. Many players who struggle around the golf courses in our great country, would envy their ability to hit the ball and play well.

For example, as a young fellow once told me about his sporty wife: he was playing a round of golf with her one weekend and she said, "Sorry dear, I lost the ball in that little hole again."

What more can one say.

The Last Word

"In the age of millennials, women's rights, and female empowerment, I hope my voice helps to encourage the next generation of great female athletes and golfers to possibly stop social injustices and prejudices from creeping into the game that I fell in love with at such a young age." – Paige Spiranac, (Golly!)

STEVE MCGREGOR

THE ENGINEERS

> *"A hole in one is amazing when you think of the different universes this white mass of molecules has to pass through on its way to the hole."* – Mac O'Grady

One wonders what goes through the mind of an engineer when he's just about to hit the ball. He is looking at effort, mass, acceleration, angle and all that side of the game. This guy has the smarts to build bridges or keep buildings upright, so his mind may be clouded by all this information and that could be what is going through his mind. Bruce wonders whether that makes him a better golfer though.

He always liked to take a golf club with him on the job.

You can just imagine how this type of player thinks. The rough, easy clean it up, put a bulldozer in. That creek. No problem, fill it up or put a bridge over it or dam it. That lot of trees in the fairway. Get rid of them! That hill, flatten it. And as for those bunkers full of sand. Well, fill 'em up. The rough encroaching on the fairway on the 10th. Put a bulldozer through the lot that should fix it.

Bruce speculates that if it were left to the engineers, golf courses would all look like the runway on Mascot airport (Sydney) in no time.

Jim is an Engineer and loves building bridges. In fact, he can't stop thinking about bridges and golf. Both are his true loves, after his ever-suffering wife Wendy and his other love, 'Tooheys Ale'. The result of all this is that Jim can get rather mixed up.

He can be out on a job with his surveyor and asked to hold the 'Measuring Rod' however, he is not thinking about anything except his golf. He looks at a creek or a dip in the land and his mind automatically wanders onto the engineering issues, if he were to start building a bridge. Holding his golf club helps.

It must detract from his ability to enjoy and even play the game.

"Golf is not, on the whole, a game for realists. By its exactitude's measurements, it invites the attention of perfectionists." Heywood Hale Broun

ACCOUNTANTS & ACTUARIES

"It's good sportsmanship to not pick up lost balls while they are still rolling." – Mark Twain, author

If an accountant or even if an actuary were to play, then no doubt they would be analysing the scorecard very closely. Imagine if he was not only an accountant but an auditor, then he would be checking his fellow player's scores, not just his own! Suspicious fellow. He couldn't help doing this, it is in his DNA. He would be checking the additions and most probably doing a complete analysis of the game. Bruce would enjoy seeing what would happen if the accountant caught any of his fellow foursome fudging the numbers.

Henry sipped his beer while doing the audit on his mates' scorecards.

The statistician would be averaging out the number of shots per game and per hole. They would be analysing all the numbers and compiling statistics on the average number of shots per game. The number of pars and so on.

After a game of golf Henry loved nothing more than to sit in the lounge with a beer and his mates' scorecards on the table before him. It is not that he does not trust his fellow golfers, it is just his desire to check all additions.

He has only found a few cards that do not meet the level of his mathematical prowess. Later he adjusts the offending card with his green inked pen and proudly shows its owner the result.

You can only imagine how the audited cards are welcomed. Some players laugh it off, others go red in the face and give him the skinny eyed look.

All the while, poor old Henry is oblivious to the emotions that his auditing stirs up.

He just doesn't want to know about the interesting quote, "Golf is a game in which you yell 'fore', shoot six, and write down five. Paul Harvey.

10

SOME OTHER GOLFER TYPES

There are so many different types of players and that is part of the reason why the game of golf is so challenging. Due to space, we have concentrated on a selection of the major types who play golf although a brief mention of some others, who deserve a special mention, are shown below.

THE RETAILER & MARKETING MAN

"Golf appeals to the idiot in us and the child. Just how childlike golf players become is proven by their frequent inability to count past five." – John Updike

The marketing executive or the advertising agent, same kind of guy or gal. Bruce can imagine, that this character approaches their game a lot different to the engineer or accountant.

His appearance is more colourful to most players. Looking a bit like an American player, they wear loud check pants, a polo shirt with the latest client's logo prominently displayed. Hair long of course and face with a sun lamp's glow. Gleaming teeth worth another overseas holiday to his dentist and a manicure set off this man's look.

For one thing, it would be a lot more fun being around this player than the other types. Their yarns are so interesting and full of the latest in the know subjects. Another feature of this player is that they take a lot of care in appearances. For example, how clean and up to date the equipment is. Who they play golf with and a custom-built electric golf cart, with a few tasteful client logos displayed.

The Marketing man also tends to look upon the game of golf, as an important venue to meet potential clients. Once one of these rare and exotic beasts is located, the golf game comes a distant second in importance. In the clubhouse, they come into their own. Free drinks, an offer of having lunch for a confidential talk and so on.

This fellow will also have some new ideas, as to how golf can be improved. He will also daydream while playing, as to how the golf club can promote the course and game. Increasing the numbers of people playing, visiting the bar and having dinner, all the lifeblood of a Golf Club manager, are mentally worked on by the Marketing Man.

The Retailer, especially those in menswear, would have the best clothes and golf equipment that you could possibly imagine. With their trained eye, they would be looking at the cut of the clothes and how tight the trousers were, due to the extra kilos gained during the Christmas break. Unfortunately, this hunger for the appearances of the game rather than the ability to play well, may lead to a lack of concentration and the player inevitably going wanders off, either mentally or physically.

The marketing man also collects his scorecards and glues them in a scrapbook. He daydreams about promoting the golf course on television. The retailer does the numbers and works out how many golfers need shirts, pants and golf paraphernalia. Their mind is never at rest and dwells very rarely on the game of golf. It is just a vehicle to network.

THE REAL ESTATE AGENT

> *"I regard golf as an expensive way of playing marbles."* – G.K. Chesterton

Bruce must say that as he has been a Real Estate Agent (Realtor) for many decades, he knows what this type of player can be like. He is the type of player that assesses the location of the golf course as a re-development site. He can visualise the expanses of greenery and fairways covered by neat complexes of townhouses, all marching along neat roads, with all wiring underground and no telegraph poles or ugly wires to ruin the aesthetics.

For example, it is often that Bruce looks out over the eleventh hole at Gordon Golf Course (NSW) and admires the view. His mouth waters when he can visualise the magnificent house built there, to take advantage of the view from the walls of glass in their living room.

Now, read on and see many of the typical golfers that you will meet on the course or in the clubhouse.

THE TEACHER & UNIVERSITY LECTURER

> *"I never learned anything from a match I won."* – Bobby Jones

These players can be terrible golfers. They are so used to teaching others, that they have difficulty in learning anything as complex as how to play a good game of golf themselves. There is a possibility that all teachers who read this are now spluttering with indignation. Consequently, as an idle question, how many of you have had golf lessons? And how many ex-teachers are golf professionals?

DOCTORS & PROFESSIONALS

"The most important shot in golf is the next one." – Ben Hogan

It is always difficult for these professionals to play a game of golf, let alone finish one. These caring and valuable members of the community, are loath to turn off their pagers or cell phones and consequently, they are called away during a game to administer to one of their patients or if needs be, a member who has succumbed to a heart attack, after a gruelling game of golf and has collapsed at the bar in the clubhouse or on the seventeenth hole.

MINISTERS OF RELIGION

"God's angels often protect his servants from potential enemies." – Billy Graham

These players find it difficult to drag themselves away from church on Sunday, but no doubt as soon as they can they don their plus fours, grab their golf kit and head for the courses. While playing, they tend to look heavenward when other players swear a little, although they silently mouth a few imprecations themselves, when things tend to go wrong.

Priests, Rabbis and Reverends can't help themselves trying to drag the Lord into assisting them with their handicaps. Just imagine the increase in the babble of prayers and so forth rising heavenward of a Sunday afternoon. Every angel must be brought in to handle the overload.

11

THE PRO SHOP

"We learn so many things from golf – how to suffer, for instance." – Bruce Lansky (a fellow sufferer)

He stood there, wanting it all.

Hands up who likes browsing through their local hardware store?

Hmm, yes all of you.

Well, another favourite pastime of a golfer, is to have a browse of the pro shop.

Not many of us can escape without buying a much needed golf glove, a new pair of golf shoes or a bag of tees.

Buying those shiny new clubs? Need those new golf shoes? Get those great new balls that promise to go further.

The solution here is to leave your credit card at home or avoid the Pro Shop and get your mates to check in for you.

Perhaps sign up for a course of sadism that the Club's Pro runs. That is the tuition for all types of golfers, be they beginners or advanced. Beware.

If there were music playing in a Pro Shop at the golf course, it would be the theme from Jaws, the movie about the giant white pointer shark. For in the dim and dark recesses of the shop the Pro lurks. If you are quick you will spot him, by his glinting eyes and white sharp teeth. He stands there motionlessly waiting to swim over and pounce.

The first you know, is when he glides towards you and in the mildest of voices says, "Do you play here often?"

If you answer, you may incur a brief lecture on the condition of the golf course, the latest golf club or equipment. All of this is leading up to the enquiry, "Do you think that you would benefit from a few golf counselling sessions?"

You see he is clever. He does not say 'Golf Lessons' because not many players like to be lectured, but 'Golf Counselling Sessions' sounds far more benign, in fact, it sounds like a bit of fun, where a few clever golf tips could be picked up.

Not so. If you are trusting enough to begin a brief Golf Counselling Session, it may turn into a nerve-wracking program, extended to ten Saturday or Sunday mornings. This is where the Pro changes the way you play golf. You end up shaking with tension and anxiety when you pick up the golf club. He changes your grip. He changes your stance, in fact, he changes everything you do, so much that you just feel uncomfortable. Once you pluck up the courage to end the sessions after the 10 weeks and try to play a game of golf, you find that you just cannot function. What before was a scrambling game where you were lucky not to have a double bogey on every hole, your game has now deteriorated to a triple bogie on each hole.

You are just not comfortable and after a few weeks, you lapse back to the way you were. Admittedly, you don't play any better, but you are back. Back to being comfortable and without the overriding feeling that you are a contortionist with a heap of worries.

Now, where were we? Ah yes, in the Pro Shop.

Recommendation: have a quick look around before you enter the shop and see if the coast is clear with no lurking Pro. Then silently enter and have a quick scan around the shelves and scoot.

"The mind messes up more shots than a body."
Tommy Bolt

12

MENTAL ATTITUDE

"One of the most fascinating things about golf is how it reflects the cycle of life. No matter what you shoot – the next day you have to go back to the first tee and begin all over again and make yourself into something." – Peter Jacobsen

Bruce using his long cue, was always a very determined though an inaccurate putter.

Many golfers will tell you that this is so important, that is, to have a positive mental attitude.

Bruce has that in bucket loads and thinks like a champion. The only problem is when he hits the ball.

Bruce once read about an American POW in Vietnam who was captured by the North Vietnamese. He was in solitary confinement for many years and to stop himself from going mad, he mentally played golf every day in his cell.

He would visualise his favourite course stateside and would start off-putting his golf bag and buggy in the car and driving to the course. And so on. He would see the shots he would make and with what club.

To cut a long story short he was thankfully eventually released and upon exiting the aircraft in the good old USA, was asked by a reporter what he would be doing when he reached home.

His reply was, that he would go and play golf on his favourite course. And that is what he did. The results were outstanding. He played to his handicap. That is the power of visualisation for you.

Now, this anecdote had a powerful message lurking in there and Bruce has not only played the full 18 holes in his mind, many times, but he has designed in theory mind you, a set of new clubs. The chapter on this warrants closer scrutiny.

SWEARING AND OTHER AIDS FOR A BETTER GAME

Hands up who have never muttered a few swear words while playing golf. Hmm, not many of you are there?

Mind you, I would say that it has never been your fault for any profanity or casting negative aspersions on the noble game.

Before reading this section of the book, you may not have realised that you can use the odd swear word to win a hole or two. The art of a good swear word can also be a help when your friend is about to tee off. This must be timed usually mid-swing.

Bruce remembers very clearly, dragging his golf buggy along and passing another golfer, obviously looking for his ball.

"Gidday, said Bruce how are you getting on?"

The other golfer stared at Bruce with a strained look on his face for an instant and replied with the immortal words, "Golf is a cow of a game!" and they parted never to be seen again.

Bruce never did see if the fellow had found his ball, but he knew deep down that the man was a sage, a philosopher of some note, with an obviously profound knowledge of the game. It was humbling.

Hitting your ball with a slice and ending up behind a tree, could bring down the wrath of heaven on the game.

Losing one's ball in the brambles that were supposed to be a well-groomed rough, is also a harrowing experience for anyone within earshot.

Conversely, if Bruce was ever fortunate enough to use his wedge and lift a ball into the cup, well, that would bring a prayer to his lips and as he cast his eyes heavenward, Bruce would fervently say, "Thank you God".

The reason for this, is that deep down in his most honest appraisal of his skills as a golfer, Bruce knew that it was not due to his prowess, but to divine intervention.

GAMESMANSHIP

If you are as intent on winning a game as is our hero Bruce then, the whole chapter devoted to this important part of the golf game is a must to read.

When the game is critically even and there are only a few holes to play and a round of drinks or a ten spot is the winnings, then any way to win is all fair in love and war .... and golf.

THE SNEEZE AND COUGH

How many times have you been tempted? We all know that a well-timed fake sneeze can also result in a loss of concentration for your fellow player. Not that Bruce would ever do this but, you never know. Mind you he would never ever try this with the 'Military Type' golfer, as he values his manhood.

No doubt the 'Joker Type' would only laugh and Bruce, who sometimes does not take the game too seriously, would have a laugh too.

THE GOTCHA

Just think of the mayhem or result, if your opponent is about to hit off or sink that important putt, when you accidentally touch them on their extended derriere, with the end of your club. Don't try this with the 'Military Man' type.

That would result in a slight change in the deviation of the ball. This course of action has to be well-timed. Note: do not do this if your opponent is a karate trained athlete or is bigger and stronger than you. Or if you do succumb to the temptation, make sure your medical cover is up to date.

DESCRIPTIVE WORDS

Now, the odd word such as "*Drat,* another bee". Or "*Golly* look at that sheila," has often proved to be a good ploy.

The odd swear word or profanity, especially if one's opponent is religious can work wonders.

Dropping a club, or even better the whole bag when your partner is about to take a shot, especially if you time it right, can also result in some spectacular results.

Moving your friend's ball, or better still, treading on it so it is deep in the soft ground can be beneficial.

Note: always remember to look the other way when your friend stares at you. Appear oblivious to any discomfort caused and so on. With a good deal of luck, the man will assume it was just a mistake.

The term 'Creative mathematics', when it comes to your scorecard – don't forget to have your rubber/eraser handy and never use a ballpoint pen, always use a pencil.

13

PROBLEM SHOTS

"Mistakes are part of the game. It's how well you recover from them, that's the mark of a great player." – Alice Cooper

How many times have you played on a course and try as you might, your ball will roll and keep on rolling until, yes, it does, it rolls right into the drink.

Bruce had the good fortune to have a game at the 'Pines Golf Course', Sanctuary Cove, Queensland, many years ago when he was young and fit. The course was perfect. It had immaculate fairways, carpet-like greens and even the expanses of water running alongside the fairways were picturesque.

Sounds great, doesn't it? Well, the game was a disaster for poor old Bruce. He would hit a ball off the tee and it would soar gracefully away and hit the fairway, just a little right of centre. It looked great. Then for some unaccountable reason, the ball did not stop. It kept on moving. It rolled faster and faster until picking up speed, it plopped into the water.

Now, this was the first hole and Bruce thought that it would improve thereafter. However, it was not to be. With every golf hole, Bruce's ball would land and then start rolling, until it splashed into the ponds, pools, seas and oceans of bloody wet stuff. Every hole he lost a ball. Until he not only lost every ball he had, but he also lost his temper.

It was a terrible day and Bruce still has nightmares about it. Our hero reckons that the Japanese architect, Tomojiro Maruyama who designed the course, must have made a mistake and all the fairways were not flat but sloped down from the middle. This chapter is similar to another section of the book, as some of these shots are mentioned in the chapter on Terminology. Basically, it is about Bruce's game and the problems he regularly contends with.

THE PREFERRED LIE

'Preferred lie' is the term that means that you as a golf player are allowed to improve your lie, without penalty on certain parts of a golf course. It's a local rule only and is also known as 'winter rules'. It's only in effect if you're informed upon arrival at the golf course. Bruce still searches for the preferred lie, as many of the courses he plays on are somewhat bumpy. Any tuft of grass will do, so he can lift the ball. Otherwise, he worries about bending the club when he digs in.

Solution: Any tuft of grass will do.

THE HOOK

Rather difficult to do this one if you want to hit a ball around a corner on a dogleg. However, when you don't want to hit a hook shot, then anything can happen. Usually, when you least expect it and with all the good intentions of that drive screaming away, straight as an arrow towards the flag, disaster occurs.

For in the blink of an eye, you will see your ball curve gracefully away in the wrong direction. Over the trees onto the next fairway.

After a lot of grumbling as you try and find your errant ball, you justify your hook, as just one of those things and it will never happen again.

As the experts describe it, a hook shot in golf is a ball that starts its trajectory on one side of the player and then curves around to the other side during flight. For right-handed players, a hook golf shot starts out to the right and swings to the left.

Solution: There is an easy cure for the Hook and that is to keep your clubface square on and not slant away even a fraction. Try and remember how you did it and use that shot on the next dogleg hole.

THE SLICE

Right-handed golfers, often have the tendency to hit the golf ball to the right--this is called a slice. In most cases, a slice occurs when you make impact with an open clubface, with either a straight or outside-in swing path. Everyone who has a tendency to slice has an identifiable problem with their swing. The answer is to concentrate and try and keep the clubface straight when you hit the ball.

Bruce, being a right-hander, occasionally finds that he slices and is rather used to looking over his right shoulder as the ball, just given a rousing thump spears away towards the trees on the side of the fairway.

Did I say occasionally hit a slice, well, to be rather candid, Bruce hits a slice more often than he would wish to.

His playing partners offer all manner of advice, but despite all their well-meaning directions, he still manages to hit a beauty onto the next fairway.

You will often come across a player kneeling and shaking his club at the sky.

Solution: Use this shot next time you are behind a large tree.

THE GRASS CUTTER

"A perfectly straight shot with a big club is a fluke."
– Jack Nicklaus

Never heard of this one, have you? Well, this is what Bruce calls his shot, when the ball is hit and instead of climbing lazily away into the blue and lobbing 200 metres towards the flag, the damn thing arcs away at about waist level and ends up grazing the top of the green grass on the fairway. In no time it has bounced a few times and comes to rest, an embarrassing 70 metres or so down the middle of the fairway.

Bruce is haunted by this shot and on his bad days, which are regrettably in the majority, starts to use a club with more loft. Instead of using say a 6-iron, he will go to an eight to try and get the ball to rise above the ground, with the forlorn hope that it will eventually end up 150 meters or so down the track, instead of becoming a fizzer of a shot which clefts the grass and comes to a stop only a few metres away.

Solution: Use this type of golf shot when you are in amongst the trees and want to get back on the fairway.

THE KANGAROO HOP

Yep, it can be assumed that everyone who has played this game, has at one time topped the ball and seen it bound away down the fairway like it was on a pogo stick. Many times, Bruce stands there with a silent prayer on his lips as the ball careens down the greenery and lands, hopefully in the middle of the fairway.

Solution: Keep your head down.

THE DUD

It is realised that you never have one of these Dud shots, so you may not need to read this section of the book. However, for those who may have more of these than they think is fair, then here is the solution.

Take up bowls, no never do that or so anything so drastic. Just persevere that is all. Read up on how to hit a better shot. Look up the Internet, read a golf book or ask the Pro at the golf shop. Invariably you will find that all the helpful suggestions, end up making your game so bad and you so uncomfortable that you end up going back to how you used to play the game.

Here is the scenario. You are for a change on the left side of the fairway. You have the flag waving away about 150 metres down the fairway and you hunch over saying to yourself, that this time it will be different.

That's right, ever an optimist you are positive that you will hit this one smoothly and well. The ball will be kissed by the face of your club and away it goes. Bounces a few times and ends up adjacent to the flag for an easy putt for a par.

So, here goes. With gritted teeth, you grasp your sweat covered handle trying to remember how to hold the damn thing properly. You then look down at the ball, which is sitting there smiling up at you waiting patiently to be hit and sent on its way. You try a practice swing that feels just great. Smooth as silk, just like Tiger does it. A ghost of a smile appears on your lips as you say, "This time it is gonna be a beauty".

You remember to commence your backswing slowly and then crisply reverse direction as you bring your club down.

Halfway down you forget to keep looking at the ball and somehow you are thinking about something else and in your mind's eye you are fishing or cleaning the car or something equally banal and swish down the club goes.

Well, instead of "click" the ball sounds an ominous "thunk" as it is hit. You hastily look down to where the ball was a split second too late, as you should have been keeping your eye on the ball. However, you are in such a hurry to see where your ball has gone that you hastily look up to see the ball flying away, but no it has already come to earth and is sitting there with an infuriating smug look on its face about 50 meters away.

Solution: Remember golf is very much a mental game. Use your head now, stay cool and concentrate.

INTO THE DRINK

If you are playing on a golf course that has a few water hazards, then this may prove to be yet another challenge to you. Bruce finds that the sight of water on the golf links tends to unnerve him.

Once Bruce was told by a depressed golf partner that he had a theory that water has a magnetic pull on a golf ball and no matter where you aim the ball it can end up splashing away mid pond, or whatever they call it when the ball sinks from sight.

In some cases the ball can skip across the surface of the pond, thus giving you a false hope that it will just keep on bouncing its way up onto firm ground. However, infuriatingly in time it loses speed and with its last bounce disappears never to be seen again.

Your ball does not usually bounce though, but with a maddeningly slow arc it soars beautifully away from your club towards the other side, but for some crazy reason, it loses momentum and yes, you guessed it, plop, into the drink.

One of the items in Bruce's golf bag is the telescopic ball retriever and just occasionally he is lucky enough to be able to retrieve his ball that can be seen just near the bank and with little difficulty can be retrieved. However, usually the Retriever is not needed, as the ball is drowning quietly somewhere deep in the dark, in the middle of the pond.

Solution: Ignore the water and try and think of it as shiny blue grass.

THE AIR SWING (A.K.A. THE PRACTICE SWING)

Just on an occasion when you have completed this litany of woe, that is trying to remember what the Golf Pro has taught you, you happen to glance down and well blow me down, the ball is still sitting there on the tee with a big dimpled grin on its face. That, my lovelies, is called an air swing.

Solution: Look cheerful, stifle your swear words and announce that it was a practice shot.

THE BUNKER SHOT

I am afraid that Bruce does not have a lot of good advice to give you on this subject.

Bruce was playing at 'Rose Bay Golf Course' or 'Royal Sydney' as it is known, as a guest of Phil Billings a well-known amateur champion. On his first drive he hit a beauty, well it was for him and off it went well over 150 metres. Regrettably 'Bilko' failed to mention that there was a massive bunker, shaped like a WWI trench just where his ball came to land.

The trench was so deep, you needed a step ladder to descend into its depths. With a sinking heart, Bruce knew that he was in for a shitty day. Only one hit of the ball and here he was at the bottom of a well, or it felt like it, looking up at the sky, but somewhere in the darkness of the trench, his ball was lying.

After a few half-hearted wacks with his sand wedge to see the ball frustratingly hit the side of the bunker and roll back down to where he was standing. Bruce's ex-friend called down to suggest, "It may be a good idea to pick it up and throw it Bruce old boy".

Basically, Bruce has lost confidence in his ability to extricate himself from the sand traps of the course and would rather hit a ball in the other direction rather than towards the gaping maw of these hazards.

Solution: Do not play with champion golfers, they will break your heart.

THE FIZZER

This is a similar shot to the Dud. This shot is usually not acknowledged by the weekend golfer. He usually counts the shot as a practice shot and either ignores it or gets out his rubber/eraser and adjusts the scorecard. Basically, it is not acknowledged, as it is never ever his fault.

Solution: Learn to invisibly amend your scorecard.

THE LOB

This is to be used when you are in that bunker or rough where you just cannot get your ball out by using any club known to man. This is when the underhand and surreptitious throw or lob comes in handy. Remember to have your club up in the air as if you have just completed a shot when your partner's head swings around to see how your ball came out of the impossible lie in the bunker.

Solution: Use your Florsheim handy toe wedge. See Chapter 7, "Designing Alternate Golf Gear".

THE LUCKY SHOT

Don't have 'em. Well, that's not strictly true, occasionally you are lucky and your ball behaves as if it was hit by Jack Nicklaus.

Solution: Say your prayers and try and appear as if you played for it and it was not a fluke.

14

DISTRACTIONS IN GOLF

"Of all the hazards, fear is the worst." – Sam Snead

DOGS ON THE COURSE

What is the attraction for dogs on a golf course? Is it all the trees, or is it all the wildlife that seems to live close by? It would be interesting to see what is walking around of a night. Perhaps an infra-red camera would do the trick. Anyhow if there is a dog, it is eventually joined by another dog and there ends up being a whole pack of them. They invariably cause the golfer to wait until they move away from the path of where the ball is to be hit. Other times they decide, in their doggy brains, that they enjoy your company and follow you around all day.

STEVE MCGREGOR

What a great dog but listen fella, first give me my ball.

Solution: Take some garlic spray for this emergency. The dog will get the message and go and pester someone else.

THE NEXT FOURSOME

"The only problem with golf is that the slow people are always in front of you and the fast people always end up behind you." – Anonymous

Now, this can be very unsettling. You are there all four of you, hunting around in the rough knowing too well that the group of players that are playing behind you are standing there with haughty looks on their faces, as you madly scramble around looking for your ball.

Eventually, you cave into the pressure and invite them, with insincere smiles, to play on through. And you try not to look as they very quickly tee off, all with smashing drives that soar away into the blue and almost bring down any low flying plane.

The other side of the coin is the four old darlings. These old girls dressed in their very best Bermuda shorts and colourful finery are tacking to and fro down the fairways as you and your comrades wait impatiently for them to finish.

Never do they call you on through, for they are oblivious to anyone else on the course. Amid screams of laughter or the odd, "Ooh, well played Gladys", the old girls' foursome are there waving their clubs, looking at the wildlife, telling tall tales and generally destroying Bruce's game.

Solution: Tell them that your ugly mate is wanting their phone number. That should speed them on their way.

KANGAROOS AND WILDLIFE

Bruce is a bit guilty here, as he is a lover of most things in wildlife and that doesn't mean nightclubs. He once played 18 holes in Mildura, a green oasis perched in the middle of a desert out west on the Victorian border. He saw a strange bird there, which he had never seen before and for many minutes wandered away to observe the creatures, while no doubt his golf partners thought him very strange. On returning home he looked up his bird book and saw that they were Apostle Birds.

An interesting fact here. They are called that because there are always 12 of them, just like the Apostles of Jesus. You don't get those birds in Sydney. Golf courses seem to attract birds, animals and regretfully hordes of insects. It must be the grass, trees and water that bring them in.

Speaking of animals, we come to Australia's own walking National symbol, the kangaroo. If anyone has played on St George's Basin Golf Course, NSW, near Jervis Bay, then you would know that there are a few mobs of grey kangaroos that have chosen the tender grass of the fairways instead of eking a subsistence life in the adjoining dry bushland.

If you hit your ball and the mob of kangaroos are lying in the way and the ball hits a big boomer (A large male) then you are firstly looking at an extra hit for your scorecard and a slight delay, until you can manage to get the boys and girls to vacate that part of the fairway so you can retrieve your ball and have your next shot.

Also, the golf course in Coonabarabran, western NSW, has a large mob of greys that live there, most probably the year around. Like St Georges Basin Golf Course these lovely animals take their time moving aside and if you manage to hit one, with your ball, then the roo just shakes its head and looks puzzled, as if to say, "What the hell was that?"

Feral pigs have been known to wander onto a golf course and can cause damage. The Golf Course rules handle this well and say that if you land in the rough caused by these pests, then you may retrieve your ball and do a drop an arms-length away from the damage.

Rabbits can also dig holes on the course and there have been cases of wild goats and deer wandering around the green grass of Australia's golf courses.

Solution: Take your camera and make the most of it.

THE ERRANT BALL

If you happen to hear the cry "fore" echoing around the course, then don't stand there and have a look. Duck. That is because a mishit ball may be heading your way.

Now, if you are the culprit and having shouted as loud as you can to warn any hapless golfer, then remember a couple of things here.

If you hit anyone, abandon your ball and move swiftly via the rough to the next fairway.

Or if you forget to yell "fore" still do it anyway and hope that they think the ball was a real fast one, when it hits them.

OR

So you were not listening or do you have a hearing problem?

At the shout of "Fore" echoing around the golf course, most golfers ignore it with the casual comment to themselves that it would not happen to them. However, they have a whinge session when the ball comes too close or hits them.

Solution: Stay alert and switch your hearing aids on.

STEVE MCGREGOR

Harold was hit a mighty wallop as the errant ball landed on his well-padded cheek.

THE WEATHER

Now, the weather can be considered a hazard. In Australia in summer, it can become very hot and the lure of a cold beer or two can lead the players to rush their game, so they can get to the clubhouse. The solution is to take a cool drink with plenty of ice.

The winter results in different problems. Rain, wind and worse, can make your game suffer. Having the correct wet weather gear and warm clothing is a great help.

We know that many golfers have combatted all these elements sometimes in the course of one game of golf. Bruce was playing at 'The Lakes' a beautiful golf course at Eastlakes, Sydney. When he hit off it was sunny with blue skies, although as the game progressed the sky darkened and the wind picked up. By the 16th hole, the skies were black and then the rain bucketed down with a brisk wind making the use of umbrellas useless.

A true golfer, Bruce and his colleagues continued and eventually finished up and made their way to the clubhouse locker room for a dry out and warm-up. This day had most of the weather types, all in the space of a few hours.

Solution: Take an umbrella for the rain. A coat for the cold, a cool drink in your handy flask. Sunscreen for the sunny day. Or if that fails retire to the 19th hole and sink a coldie or two.

INSECTS AND OTHER NASTIES

These pests can make your life miserable and golfers are not immune to them either.

You are about to take a swing and a fly somehow ends up in your mouth. Or in your eye or settled on your nose and so on. All of these are rather off-putting. In summer, the flies can make you miserable. They gather in a cloud on your back and with every movement of your body, they take off as aircraft from a carrier on a bombing raid and invade your face.

Thankfully, there are various sprays to use, to spray your face and arms, to fend off the depredations of these irritating creatures.

On various golf courses surface water, or adjacent marshland can harbour masses of mosquitoes. They usually take over from the flies on sun-down. As with flies, there are various personal sprays that can be used to combat them.

Imagine this, there you are. It is hot. You sit down to ease your aching back and pull out your cold drink that by this time has become tepid and unpleasant. Suddenly, you feel a sting and you look down to see that there are a host of ants swarming around your golf shoes and climbing up your legs.

The depredations of Australia's wildlife can truly be a problem. Though we can imagine playing in Africa and combatting lions and elephants would be somewhat more of a problem.

Solution: Mortein's 'Aerogard', mate, take a can with you and spray yourself liberally before the game. That should zap the little critters.

NATURAL HAZARDS

Tree in the way? Stuck in a gully? In the coil of hose left by the groundsman? Yep, we have all been there, done that.

So what's the plan, Bruce? Well, Bruce knows that some of these hazards are alright and you just pick up the ball and drop it out of the way, without losing a point. Others, however, are not so easy to literally get around. This is where the Engineer type player comes into his own.

The Military man can't blow it up but the Engineer can work out the best angle to get around that hazard. Bruce always defers to his friend, the Engineer, rather than the gifted amateur in these types of cases. The gifted amateur will try and turn Bruce into a better player and that will not happen, so Bruce looks for the easy way out.

Bruce just handed the Engineer his trusty hatchet, that he just happened to have in his bag, and in no time the way was free for Bruce to chip out to safety. Okay, I exaggerated a little. Although, it could have happened. Anything can happen on a golf course.

Solution: Be creative and don't take those hazards lying down. You must be more proactive.

GOLF – THE TRUE STORY

WATER HAZZARD

Bruce refused to walk away and leave his ball.

Yes, we have already covered this, but Bruce has demanded we put it in again. You see he is one of those golfers that is drawn to water, literally!

Solution: Unlike Bruce, give in and leave the ball there for the kids to find when they collect golf balls. Get your rubber/eraser out and adjust your scorecard. No one will notice.

BIRDS (PRETTY GIRLS)

One could adapt blinkers, but the golfers are known for their positive thinking and usually wander over to have a good look. They will tell themselves and whoever is in earshot, that they are doing this to see if they can help. The result is, that their concentration is shot and their game is a litany of woe.

Solution: Keep your head down or wear blinkers.

BIRDS (THE FEATHERED SORT)

The magpie is usually a problem on the golf course. At nesting times, mother magpie decides that any golfer that strays too close to her nest or chicks will be the recipient of a dive-bombing exercise. This results in an amazing peck of their heavy beak to the head. It feels like you have been hit by a rock, thrown at you. However, the beak of a magpie with a strong neck movement behind it results in a sore head.

Solution: Keep your hat on. Or stick eyes on the back of your hat that keeps them away.

MOBILE PHONES, THE WIFE'S THREATS, ETC.

Irritating isn't it when your partner spends more time talking on his cell phone or texting, than talking to you. Over 18 holes this behaviour can start to get you down and you find that you are starting to boil. You look longingly at the water feature, with the idea of snatching the offending phone from his ear and throwing it into the lake. Or perhaps surreptitiously pilfering it and digging a hole in the bunker on the 15th and look mystified when he starts hunting around for his lost love.

Solution: Tread on said phone by 'mistake'.

YOUR PARTNER'S ANTICS

See Chapter 9, People Who Play Golf, 'The Clown' – yes, this is a hazard alright. Most golfers at one time, feel like clobbering their partner harder than they hit the ball and that is usually for incessant talking, crumby jokes and attempts at gamesmanship and so on.

Solution: Don't get angry get even.

PASSING TRAFFIC

Bruce remembers only too well, hitting a ball off the second tee at Pennant Hills Golf Course, NSW, and seeing it slice away and bounce down the main road, adjacent to the course before bouncing off an oncoming car's windscreen. The answer to this was as you may think, stop slicing.

When Bruce noticed the angry motorist stopping and exiting his car, he had the presence of mind to turn his back on the driver and pointed at something, hoping like mad that the irate motorist would drive off.

Solution: Run and hide.

NIGHT – DARKNESS FALLS

Okay, you are still out there chasing balls and grumbling away. Those 18 holes have taken longer than you thought. But you're not going to give in! You want your monies worth! No bloody way will you give in!

Solution: Never surrender. Find that pesky ball and oh yes, take a flashlight with you.

ABNORMAL GROUND CONDITIONS

So it has been raining. The course is waterlogged and there you are tramping around with mud and slush covering your clean new boots.

However, you know, with a sinking heart that many more problems are coming your way. You will experience very slow putting, which will guarantee to increase your blood pressure. Also when you drive, your ball will hit the ground and instead of bouncing along merrily, to add another 50 metres of length, digs in and stubbornly lies there and thus inviting you to dig it out.

Solution: Dig the ball out and stop grumbling. It may be sunny next week.

BEERS (OR ANY OTHER ALCOHOL FOR THAT MATTER)

Beers first thing at 7.00 am is more than a hazard. You may have been able to kick off your golf day like that when you were in your twenties, but now in your autumn years, anything like that would lead to disaster.

Solution: If you are going to have a drink then eat a hearty breakfast first.

15

THE 19TH HOLE

"I don't often play golf but when I do I drink too much." – Anonymous

You are halfway through the eighteenth hole and the clubhouse is there at the end of the fairway, gleaming in the sunlight. You know that within its portals lies the place of your dreams, the bar.

It is with great difficulty, you bring your mind back to the game. You try to forget your aching back, the lost golf balls, the mishits and hope that the Great Creator, will forgive you for making a few unwarranted changes on your scorecard.

You concentrate, as you know that the anguish will be all over and your reward is beckoning. A cold beer should do the trick.

Knowing full well, that you will do it all over again next week. You will fervently believe that you will have no hooks or slices. You will avoid the little lake, that usually swallows your golf ball and Heaven forbid, you will not need your rubber/eraser for the scorecard.

Bruce reckons that having a cold beer with the boys is one of the reasons why he took up golf in the first place. He does so enjoy sitting at the bar, in the clubhouse quaffing a few coldies, as he swaps a few fibs with his mates.

Afterwards, he makes his way home to recover from a very long day.

Bruce was tired, cold, wet and had a few beers aboard. He will do it all again next week.

There you have it "Golf – The True Story" is a book that is chock full of helpful hints on your favourite game. With all the champion class tips contained in this book, you cannot fail to look at the game of golf with new eyes. Bruce will not be the first golfer to give advice, after all, it is the cheapest coin in the realm. He is an optimist though, and believes fervently, that this valuable book will lead to a great improvement not only in your game but in your attitude to playing well.

Remember what the great Bobby Jones said, "The secret of golf is to turn three shots into two."

ABOUT THE AUTHOR

Steve McGregor is the author of several books including *Adventures of a Jackeroo, The Adventures of Bruce from Bondi,* and *Golf: The True Story.* He derives great enjoyment from furnishing his stories with unique and funny illustrations, peppering his prose with humorous observations. When he isn't writing or creating you can find him on the golf course or walking his dog.

He has many interests and like the gormless hero, Bruce, in his books still shoots with the 18th Battalion each year. He also is a sought after public speaker and presents on subjects as diverse as Warfare in Ancient Egypt, Weapons of the American Civil War and the WWII fighter aircraft, the Spitfire, and much more.

Steve is married to Glynne, also an accomplished artist, and they live on the North Shore of Sydney with their dog Bonnie.

www.ingramcontent.com/pod-product-compliance
Lightning Source LLC
Chambersburg PA
CBHW050312010526
44107CB00055B/2209